Focus on the Language Learner

Approaches to identifying and meeting the needs of second language learners

Elaine Tarone and
George Yule

Oxford University Press

Oxford University Press
Walton Street, Oxford OX2 6DP

Oxford New York Toronto
Delhi Bombay Calcutta Madras Karachi
Petaling Jaya Singapore Hong Kong Tokyo
Nairobi Dar es Salaam Cape Town
Melbourne Auckland

and associated companies in
Berlin Ibadan

Oxford and *Oxford English* are trade marks of
Oxford University Press

ISBN 0 19 437061 5
© Elaine Tarone and George Yule 1989

First published 1989
Second impression 1991

Typeset in Linotron Sabon by Hope Services, Abingdon
Printed in Hong Kong

The authors and publishers would like to thank the following for
permission to reproduce the material below:

Cambridge University Press for the extract from K. Morrow and
K. Johnson: *Communicate 1*

The authors for the extract from M. Eisenstein and J. Bodman:
' "I very appreciate": expressions of gratitude by native and non-
native speakers of American English' in *Applied Linguistics* 7

Longman Group UK Limited for extracts from W. Mackey:
Language Teaching Analysis

The authors for the extract from G. Yule, J. Yanz, and A. Tsuda:
'Investigating aspects of the language learner's confidence: an
application of the theory of signal detection' in *Language Learning* 35

Contents

Preface

This is a book which was inspired by the work of second language teachers as they attempted to *identify and meet the local needs of the learners in their classrooms.* It is consequently not a book which presents a single view of how language learning takes place, nor does it promote one global solution for all language teaching problems. Rather, it offers a range of ideas, techniques, and procedures which, in different classroom situations, have provided new insights concerning variability in learner language and the learning process, prompted different types of teaching activities, and fostered a qualitative change in the classroom experiences of many learners. *The common theme throughout all this work is a focus on first identifying the local needs of particular groups of second language learners and then working toward meeting those needs.*

We are aware that, at many points in the following pages, practicing teachers with a busy schedule will wonder where they could find the time to carry out some of the types of investigations proposed as useful in identifying learner needs. It is not our intention that this should be a concern at all. Quite simply, we offer some ideas and some techniques which we have found to be useful. Take what you think may be useful for your particular situation. Ignore what you disagree with, or what you suspect will be too difficult to implement given your current teaching situation.

Basically, we hope that anyone in the field of second language teaching who only has enough time to read this book, or sections of it, will at least gain something: a better understanding of how the process of identifying learners' needs can have a beneficial effect on the process of attempting to meet those needs. We feel that this understanding, in itself, is valuable.

Acknowledgments

A great many friends, colleagues, and students have helped us in many ways in the preparation of this book. We would especially like to thank Eric Nelson for his careful reading of, and comments on, an early manuscript. We would also like to acknowledge the help and support of Grant and Rachel Abbott, Lisa Berwick, Hugh W. Buckingham, Pam Couch, Jack Damico, Lyn Del Caro, Deborah Feldman, Judy Fuller, Susan Gillette, Deniz Gokcora, Wayne Gregory, Kathryn Hanges, Kristin Hershbell, Paul Hoffman, Alison Houck, Keith Holmes, Wayne Jacobson, Lois Malcolm, Karen Sorensen, Michele Trufant, Atsuko Tsuda, and Jerry Yanz. We would also like to acknowledge our debt to many other professionals in the field whose names do not appear here, but who will recognize the influence of their contributions, often given generously, but anonymously, in professional meetings and critical reviews.

PART ONE

Basic issues

Introduction

Why is it that language teachers never seem to be quite satisfied with any one methodology or any one set of teaching materials? Why, for example, is it extremely common to observe language teachers spending a great deal of preparation time patching together lesson material from various sources, constructing their own readings and exercises, and then busily working with a photocopier or duplicator? It cannot be claimed that there are no available textbooks for language teaching. On the contrary, there is a wealth of commercially produced language teaching material and yet, even when supplied with the most recent of textbooks —often chosen after extensive consultation and review by experts— language teachers are still to be observed busily changing sections or creating additional material. In fact, one extremely experienced and very competent teacher of English as a Second Language (ESL) recently told us: 'Even if I were using a text I had written myself only last year, I wouldn't use it without modification.'

What can account for this seeming perversity? It is our belief that the answer lies in the fact that no two foreign language classes are ever the same, and that language teachers recognize this. In order to successfully teach a second or foreign language to adults, teachers recognize that, at a very practical level, they must constantly adjust their methods and materials on the basis of their identification of the *local needs of their students*. If those perceived needs differ with each new class, then it ceases to be surprising that teachers seem to spend extra time preparing additional materials specifically designed for each new group. In a sense, then, the source of dissatisfaction among language teachers is their own intuitive awareness that there is not one fixed methodology which will work with all students, and that there is no one set of materials which will guarantee successful learning for all. Indeed, perhaps the most frustrating experience for many novice teachers on entering the language teaching profession is the discovery that there simply isn't a prescribed set of procedures which they will learn and then implement in the classroom. What the novices have to learn is that there exists a wide range of alternatives, both in teaching methods and in types of materials, and that the way to make their own lessons work effectively with their own particular students is to develop the ability to select from those alternatives (or even to create novel approaches) in accordance with what they perceive to be their students' needs. The teacher trainer must somehow impart to the novice a clear understanding of this process.

However, this process may also be a source of frustration for many experienced language teachers. They know that they do in fact work out ways to provide their students with appropriate lesson material, yet often they are not quite sure about how they come to achieve this, and they have great difficulty articulating the processes involved. It is a frustration which results from having a good intuitive sense of what will work, but not being able to explain why in any objective sense.

We hope that, in the course of this book, we shall be able to present arguments and illustrate procedures which will make sense in terms of language teachers' intuitions and which will not only provide guidance to the novice, but will in effect provide experienced teachers with ways to become more articulate about their own experience in the classroom so that they can say why they believe their approach worked. We shall try to show that the processes of identifying what the students need to know, investigating what the students do and do not know already, and gaining insight into how the students perceive their own abilities—far from being the purview of the expert outsider—are at the very heart of the successful classroom teacher's activities in second or foreign language instruction. In so doing, we hope we shall provide novice language teachers with guidance in a complex field and at the same time provide experienced language teachers with a number of incentives toward a greater sense of professionalism and a firmer conviction that what they do can have a powerful impact on the process of second language acquisition. In short, we would like to minimize some of the frustration and dissatisfaction mentioned above by providing language teachers with:

- a means to define their own teaching goals by working out the needs of their students in relatively specific terms
- practical methods, with accompanying illustrations of materials, to identify different aspects of their students' needs
- a sense of personal and professional security in their own ability to make decisions concerning the methods and materials used with a particular group of students, and to support these decisions with relevant data ·
- a means of critically assessing the claims of theorists in the field of second language acquisition by looking at their own data derived from their own practical experience with their particular group of learners.

This book, then, is *not* designed for curriculum developers interested in doing large-scale needs analysis projects: it is intended for classroom language teachers interested in improving their ability to analyze the needs of particular groups of learners in order to make practical teaching decisions. To this end, we will now look at some aspects of what is known about the language learning process itself.

1 The learning part

A major source of frustration for novice language teachers surfaces when they try to decide, often in advance, which view of the language learning process should be adopted as most suitable for meeting the needs of their students. From teacher preparation courses on language teaching methodology and materials, they will most likely have been provided with an array of different points of view, some of which are in direct conflict with others. For example, should they choose to follow a model of inductive learning, providing lots of examples, plenty of practice, and a minimum of explanation? Or should they start with a clear explanation, followed by a few examples and the practice formats associated with a deductive learning model? Should they try to follow the example of some older and very experienced language teacher who insists that, despite all the criticisms, Audiolingual methodology is still the most effective? Or should they believe the powerful claims made by advocates of more innovative methods, such as Total Physical Response, Counseling-learning, and the Natural Approach, that such methods produce more rapid, longer-lasting second language skills? These are just a few examples of the types of questions which arise when the consideration of what should be done in language teaching is undertaken without taking the needs of some particular group of learners into account. They are, in a sense, unanswerable questions if no information is available on who the learners are, what they know and have experienced already, and what they might need to know. The process of getting that information is the subject of the central chapters of this book.

The learning process

Before investigating the learner's needs, however, we may briefly consider some questions which relate to the teacher's needs, in the sense that many teachers do want to know which view (if any) of the learning process is the most appropriate for language teaching. After all, they may have noted that there is strong disagreement between one school of thought and another, to the extent that each claims that it is correct and the others are wrong. The teacher wants to know which one is *really* correct. A classic example of such a disgreement would be the apparent conflict between the different views of the second language acquisition process proposed by Krashen (1981) and McLaughlin (1978). Let us consider the general ideas put forward in this debate as representative of a larger and fairly long-standing conflict that has troubled most language teachers at one time or another. In relatively non-technical terms, we can say that Krashen claims that the key aspect of second language acquisition is an unconscious process resulting from experience in using the language, and that this process is not directly benefitted by the conscious learning of, for example, grammatical rules. The explicit learning of rules during classroom instruction, he argues, only provides a means of 'monitoring' output and does not easily convert into 'acquired', or automatic, language ability. In contrast, McLaughlin argues that learning in a conscious way in a classroom setting should not be treated as a peripheral aspect of language acquisition and that learned aspects of the second language can become automatic processes in the use of the language.

Reading of these opposing views, language teachers face a dilemma in trying to decide how to organize lessons. They typically have to decide on very practical matters such as the following: 'Will explicit teaching of the form and structure of English relative clauses to a Chinese student eventually have any direct influence on that student's ability to produce and understand English relative clauses in a fairly automatic way?' One theorist suggests that it will not, the other says that it may. Putting theoretical positions aside for the moment, we might suggest one possible way of answering this question, as follows: 'It depends on the student.' Interestingly, this type of answer has some support from the work of another writer on second language acquisition, John Schumann.

Schumann (1983) argues that Krashen and McLaughlin may actually be basing their arguments on their own personal, and quite different, language learning experiences. If, as a learner, your experience has been one in which you believe that formal grammatical instruction has enabled you to become a relatively proficient user of the second language, then you would tend to agree with McLaughlin and feel that Krashen was requiring you to deny your own experience. If you have become proficient via use of the second language in a situation where there was little or no formal grammatical instruction, then you would feel that your experience has been accurately captured by Krashen's proposal. From this perspective, both Krashen and McLaughlin are right, or as Schumann puts it:

> Krashen and McLaughlin's views can coexist as two different paintings of the language learning experience—as reality symbolized in two different ways. Viewers can choose between the two on an aesthetic basis, favoring the painting which they find to be phenom-enologically true to their experience. Neither position is correct; they are simply alternate representations of reality.
> (Schumann 1983: 55)

It seems clear that researchers cannot at present agree upon a single view of the learning process which can safely be applied wholesale to language teaching. Another insight which follows from Schumann's observation is that teachers should recognize the important influence of their own language learning experience on their views of the learning process in general, and also remain aware of the effect that their students' previous language learning experience will have on their views of language learning. We shall return to this issue of the students' expectations later in the chapter.

The conclusion reached by Schumann tends to concentrate on the positive aspects of both views of the second language acquisition process. We should also remember that there appear to be disadvantages associated with both approaches. Krashen points out that a learner who is concerned with producing grammatically correct language may become hesitant, lack fluency, and generally sacrifice communicative effectiveness in using the language in order to try to achieve formal accuracy. By implication, then, a learning experience which is dominated by classroom instruction on the rules and correct form of the language may interfere with the ability to actually use the language in interactive situations. If it is the case that the interactive use of the language does, in itself, contribute to the development of greater proficiency, then the formal learning experience may have a negative effect on the student's long-term development of language proficiency. This has to be considered a serious problem, and one which many language teachers will recognize from their experience with some students who, for example, can provide grammatical descriptions of English relative clauses, and who can easily perform sentence combination exercises in the classroom to create relative clauses, yet whose poor spoken English performance does not seem to put these skills into practice.

The opposite effect has been noted (by, for example, Higgs and Clifford 1982) as one of the major disadvantages of a language learning experience which primarily consists of language use for communicative purposes, without a great deal of attention being paid to grammatical accuracy. The tendency in this type of situation is for the learner to become relatively fluent and successful in terms of message communication, but to produce consistently inaccurate grammatical or phonological forms of the language. The long-term effects of such a learning experience can be just as debilitating with regard to proficiency. Many teachers will recognize such learners as ones who do not seem to change or improve their ability to produce grammatical forms despite extended periods of instruction. Moreover, their apparently high degree of communicative effectiveness in the spoken language is rarely matched by their scores in proficiency tests or in producing written work. It has been suggested that such learners have become relatively successful communicators using ungrammatical forms which become 'fossilized' and which are not amenable to change. This also has to be considered a serious problem which, as Higgs and Clifford have pointed out, can interfere with the career objectives of many language learners.

Learners' aims

That last observation brings us back to a consideration of the language learner's needs. Neither of the approaches to language learning we have just discussed is *necessarily* disdvantageous when considered from the point of view of a specific group of learners' particular aims in learning a second language. If a group of Spanish speakers set out to learn English, in a Spanish school, with the fairly general aim of developing sufficient knowledge of how the English language works to enable them to make sense of occasional written publications in English, and have no intention of spending any time in, or taking part in the life of an English-speaking community, then their needs may be quite adequately served by courses which concentrate on written materials, with accompanying grammar and vocabulary exercises. Alternatively, if another group of Spanish speakers, attending the same school, are planning to move to the United States and to take part, on a day-to-day basis, in conversational interaction with their American neighbors, then their needs might be better served by courses which concentrate on spoken materials designed to foster the interactive use of conversational English. This type of distinction based on learners' aims is relatively well-known, and serves, when the very specialized aims of a group can be identified, as the rationale for the whole enterprise known as Language for Special Purposes (LSP).

What such a broadly-based distinction easily obscures, however, is that learners' aims, in terms of life or career, are not always so readily characterized at any one point in time, nor do they necessarily remain constant. It also neglects the fact that both types of learner necessarily have something in common—what Widdowson (1983) describes as the need to develop the capacity to creatively exploit, in novel situations, the linguistic knowledge provided in their special training. The notion of 'learners' aims' is complex. And, for large numbers of language learners, the external purposes for which they are learning the second language may be very poorly defined. The learners may have quite general purposes which will require a variety of language-using skills and consequently the 'best' type of learning experience for them cannot always be determined from the perspective of highly specific purposes. Moreover, relatively few teachers are ever provided with detailed background information on their students' aims in taking a second language course. A questionnaire handed out by the teacher in class may reveal that, within a single group, individual aims are quite varied.

(A very common aim, we suspect, is simply limited to passing the examination at the end of the course.)

As a result, decisions about how to present the 'best' learning experience for a group of students inevitably depend on the individual teacher's ability to work out what those students appear to need, while also remaining aware of what they expect to happen in the learning situation. As Widdowson (1983) points out, such a teacher may define these students' needs in terms of processes of learning rather than solely in terms of end goals and purposes.

Learners' expectations

Some adult learners have quite powerful preconceptions about the form a language learning experience should take. We simply cannot ignore the fact that many learners are used to an educational setting in which teachers overtly control the activities of the group in a relatively formal manner, emphasize the memorization of grammatical rules and vocabulary, often via mechanical procedures such as repetition and rote learning, administer frequent achievement tests, and generally require their students to maintain a passive and subordinate role. If students from such a background are thrust into a much more informal setting in which the teacher assumes a less authoritarian role, expects interactive group work among students, does not encourage memorization or administer achievement tests, and generally acts as if students should be responsible for their own learning, then they may feel that their teacher just doesn't know how to do the job properly. Such a reaction may have quite a negative effect on a student's ability to derive any benefit from the learning experience.

Teachers' reactions to such learner expectations can take various forms. They can ignore a single student's initial unwillingness to take part and trust that he or she will see the benefit of their methods as the course proceeds. Faced with a large group's hostility, however, teachers may be forced to abandon their planned methods and, in a sense, give the 'customers' what *they* think they need. These two reactions are examples of what Powell and Taylor (1985) have termed the *fight 'em* or *join 'em* solutions to this aspect of meeting learners' needs. A third response, called *channel 'em*, is what many teachers aim for in such situations. This is a compromise position in which both teacher and student can fulfill their expectations of what counts as an effective learning experience. In practice, this compromise can take many forms. For example, it is possible to begin a class on English relative clause structures as if it were a traditional grammar lesson, with the teacher encouraging those students with previous knowledge of the structures to contribute to the whole group's awareness of the formal properties of this aspect of the English language. However, rather than proceed to a traditional grammar exercise such as sentence combining, the teacher can lead the group to consider what the function of such structures is in the use of the language. The teacher can also provide exercise material which forces the students to create and manipulate such structures in a way which depends on their communicative function (for example, identifying referents, or distinguishing between similar referents). Alternatively, the teacher may begin the lesson with a communicative task such as a narrative in which a number of different referents have to be identified and distinguished at different points, tape-record the spoken narratives of one or more students, and then later use the tape-recording as source material for a discussion of how well the speaker used the language to identify the referents involved. Such a discussion can then include a consideration of whether the relative clauses used were well-formed or not, whether a single adjective would have been better than the full relative clause which the speaker used, how reduced relative clauses can cause confusion, and so on. The point of this brief consideration of compromise solutions is to try to draw attention to the ways in which the teacher's perception of learners' needs (for example, more flexible use of the spoken language in functional terms) do not have to be seen as conflicting with learners' expectations (for example, analysis of the grammar in formal terms).

The eclectic approach

Partially as a result of seeking such compromise solutions to meet the perceived needs of language learners and partially as a result of a greater sense of individualism among teachers who are resisting adherence to any single methodology, there has emerged a general movement toward eclecticism, of picking and choosing some procedures from one methodology, some techniques from another, and some exercise formats from yet another. This approach seems to us to represent a reasonable response from the practicing teacher who is typically concerned, on a day-to-day basis, with whether specific procedures or exercises seem to 'work' well for a particular group of students, rather than with whether the lesson format might fit into some theory. It seems to be less common to find teachers trying to make sure that their lessons follow some theoretical model and taking on trust that the students will get something out of them because the theory said they should. Eclecticism has at times been criticized, particularly by advocates of one methodology or another, as resulting in a hodgepodge of conflicting classroom activities assembled on whim rather than upon any principled basis. In fact, effective eclecticism cannot be achieved without effort, and cannot be based on ignorance. It places a great deal of responsibility on the individual teacher's ability to choose appropriate procedures and materials according to some principle or some set of principles. Making that choice, we will contend, has to result from an identification of the learner's needs. We have taken the view, in preparing this book, that the best perspective from which to consider those needs comes not from a global theory but from an investigation of the highly localized situation of the teacher's classroom. Since that situation is influenced by so many factors, often reflecting administrative rather than pedagogical convenience, the teacher's personal contribution to the learner's experience has to derive from an individual reaction to the status of a group of other individuals. This approach involves a philosophy of *local solutions to local problems* and has to remain sufficiently flexible to allow recognition of a great deal of variation in the nature of the language learning experience.

If we can accept the concept of variation in the nature of the learning experience, we should also be sensitive to a similar phenomenon in the nature of language. A language can be treated as a set of fixed forms and structures which can be isolated, in grammatical or functional terms, and taught separately. However, such a treatment, as we shall argue in the following section, will provide an extremely misleading perspective on what it is that language users actually make use of and, consequently, what the target repertoire of learners ought to be.

2   The language part

It is difficult to imagine an investigation of the needs of language
learners which could be undertaken without some attention being paid
to the nature of the language being learned. Attention of this sort is
usually a form of linguistic analysis which is carried out, however
informally, by practicing language teachers all the time. They talk about
texts and exercises which have 'easy' or 'difficult' vocabulary, comment
on the grammatical and phonological errors their students produce, and
occasionally argue about the sequence in which different aspects of the
language should be presented. These discussions usually include
linguistic terms such as 'noun' and 'verb' for the categorization of word-
forms, 'vowel' or 'diphthong' for sound segments, and 'passive' or
'interrogative' for sentence structures. They may also include linguistic
rules of the type: 'You must add –s to the third person singular present
tense of the verb in English', or 'Questions using the English verb *to be*
must be formed by inverting the subject and the verb'. Being able to use
these linguistic terms and to define these linguistic rules is normally
assumed to be an essential part of the professional knowledge of the
practicing language teacher.

   It is, however, quite remarkable that the linguistic terminology used
by language teachers, as illustrated above, continues to evoke categories
and relationships which are essentially those of traditional grammar.
Most practicing teachers who talk about the language of their
classrooms seem to share a vocabulary which has more in common with
Jespersen (1933) than with Chomsky (1965). Yet, any language teacher
who has taken a linguistics course within the last fifteen years or so will
most likely have studied some version of Chomsky's transformational-
generative grammar and, in the process, will have been explicitly discouraged from thinking of English grammatical rules in the traditional
way. Other language teachers who have received training in courses
presented by structural linguists will have been informed that traditional
definitions such as 'a noun is a word used for naming something' are, at
worst, inaccurate and, at best, quite vacuous. In other words, despite a
lot of argument, and also ridicule, directed against traditional grammar,
it continues to serve as the day-to-day basis of the language teacher's
approach to linguistic analysis. Is this simply another example of
perversity, or might there be something that practicing language
teachers know about language analysis which linguists have missed? We

might begin by noting that there are some good reasons why the analytic methodologies of current mainstream linguistics have been largely rejected by language teachers.

Linguistic analysis

The study of language, as practiced by many contemporary linguists, is based on a commitment to the kind of analytic rigor typical of work in the physical sciences. The common definition of linguistics as 'the scientific study of language' and of language as 'a rule-governed system' should consequently be treated as serious statements concerning both analytic methodology and the nature of the object under investigation. For example, in adopting a 'scientific' or, in some cases, a 'mathematical' framework within which to work, many linguists have to adhere to very rigorous criteria in determining the adequacy of their analyses. When they produce a rule of grammar, for example, they have to remember that a scientific 'rule' must be 100 per cent accurate and admit no exceptions. One counter-example to a claimed rule of this type is considered sufficient to invalidate it. Consequently, linguistic rules of the scientific type have to be treated as categorial, or exceptionless, not unlike the 'laws' of physics. In order to derive these rules, the analyst has to treat language as a static object and assume that it is totally regular and unconnected to any extraneous contextual factors. By adopting this approach, with several other related constraints, a number of linguists (for example, Chomsky 1965) have been able to produce quite powerful models of linguistic analysis in the areas of generative syntax and formal semantics.

However, many language teachers who have taken courses in these areas have come away with the uneasy feeling that such an approach does not seem to have any direct relevance to the phenomena they are interested in. They may note that the data are so restricted that they seem to exclude a large proportion of what occurs in the daily use of language, and that the individual's communicative purposes have no role to play in what is essentially a system of automatic rules relating one form to another. In short, what teachers tend to find in formal grammars is an analysis of the language of a pre-programmed automaton, whereas what they seek is a way of looking at the language of the ordinary human in action.

The language teacher sees that, in daily language use, the human seems to operate with 'rules' which may be best characterized as 'probabilistic', rather than categorial. In the user's experience, a particular structure will tend to be used in a recognizable context *more often than not*. Hence, a good operating 'rule' will be very effective for the user if it is correct just eighty per cent of the time. Intimately connected with this is the experience of variation, that is, that humans do not use the same language in the same way all the time. Yet this variation is not random. It tends to be the case that the choice of one form over another will be determined by recognizable aspects of the situation of use. Finally, the language user, unlike the automaton, uses and manipulates linguistic form to convey intended meanings. For the human, language is a functional system in which linguistic form serves a primarily communicative purpose.

Consequently, to look at language-in-use, the language teacher needs to have an analytic approach which will accommodate the fact that the primary categories may be functional rather than formal, that there will be variation in the realization of those categories, and that the 'rules', or organizing principles on which the system operates, may be probabilistic in nature.

Viewing language in this way, one may be able to recognize part of the appeal of traditional grammar. Categories like 'noun' are usually defined in notional terms which apply to the most typical members of a set. That is, when you say that 'a noun is a word used for naming something', you are describing the *function* typically performed by a set of linguistic items. In other words, you are describing what it is used for rather than what its formal properties must be. The definition of a category like 'pronoun' as 'a word which stands in place of a noun' cannot be treated as entirely accurate in English. This is a probabilistic rule for identifying pronoun function. It says that the set of forms called pronouns will be found to stand in place of nouns more often than not, but, of course, there will be exceptions. For example, in the expression *it rains a lot in November*, we would identify the word *it* as a pronoun, but would have some difficulty saying which noun it stands in place of. The concept of 'exceptions' is another feature of traditional grammar and one way in which aspects of variation are incorporated. A typical entry for a 'rule' will consist of a general statement, covering the majority of cases, followed by a number of cases, or 'exceptions', where the generalization does not apply. In other words, traditional grammar goes some way toward encoding the kind of things the language user is sensitive to and, hence, provides a relatively informal method of linguistic analysis which teachers seem to find useful.

Rules and explanations

Despite the fact that traditional descriptive grammar has remained a constant pedagogical resource, there has always been a tendency among teachers to want to take the rather loose, informal, descriptive lines and tighten them up considerably. After all, a system which is functionally driven, probabilistic in its organization, and subject to extensive variation does present rather unwieldy and unsatisfying subject matter.

One obvious way in which this tightening up of the system is carried out comes in the form of statements on what form the language *should* take. In this process, the grammar is stripped of some of its descriptive lines and becomes 'prescriptive'. Prescriptive rules may range from fairly accepted ones like 'You must use -*s* on third person singular present tense verbs' to ones like 'You must not end a sentence with a preposition', which are commonly ignored by native speakers. Prescriptive rules tend to distort the observable facts of the language to comply with some social precepts, just as a generative approach can distort via compliance with some mathematical precepts. Thus, the effect of 'tightening up' the description of actual language-in-use tends to have a distorting effect on what is being described. In more subtle ways, this effect can be discerned in the rules and explanations which often turn up in the course of classroom instruction.

By way of illustrating this last point, let us imagine a class in which English indirect speech constructions are being presented. A 'rule' of tense harmony is invoked to show that, when the reporting verb is in the past tense, the present tense of the direct speech verb must be changed to the past tense in indirect speech. Students are given an exercise format for practicing this 'rule' which involves seeing (1) in the example below and being asked to produce (2):

1 **Eric:** 'Susan is ill.'
   What did Eric say?
2 Eric said that Susan was ill.

What the student learns in such exercises is that the present tense form *is* in (1) must be changed to *was* in (2) to achieve tense harmony with the reporting verb *said*. Unfortunately, this process is presented in our imaginary class as the only structural option available to English speakers if they wish to report the information in (1). Yet this type of exercise, we would like to suggest, is not based on a categorial rule of English, but on a probabilistic one. We assume that the generalization of the tense harmony rule came about because the past tense form in *Susan was ill* was observed more often in such constructions than the present tense form in (3):

3 Eric said that Susan is ill.

Despite the absence of tense harmony, this is a grammatical English sentence, differing from (2) only to the extent that the person making the report has taken a different view on the relevant time of the relationship between *Susan* and *ill*. So, when you have received a telephone call from Eric concerning Susan's health, and you are asked what Eric said, you have a choice in making your report and that choice will be determined by your view of the relevant time of Susan's being ill.

This description of what may be involved in the use of one tense rather than another in reported speech brings up an important pedagogical issue—the problem of 'explanation'. We can certainly present language learners with examples of reported speech in English and illustrate *how* the language works. We can even emphasize, in a number of our examples, that there is a higher probability of one form rather than another occurring. However, a problem arises when the learner asks *why* a particular form is used. For many teachers, and learners too, the most comfortable answer seems to be the statement of some 'rule', such as the 'tense harmony rule' in English indirect speech. There are at least two dangers in this apparent solution. The first is that language teachers do not always have an explanatory rule to offer. They may not have heard of a rule to explain a particular phenomenon, or they may not even be sure that an accurate description of a rule exists to cover a particular case. To take one example, what is the explanatory rule which accounts for the acceptability of (4) below, but not (5)?

4 They told me to wait.
5 *They suggested me to wait.

Few teachers would be able to provide a simple, accurate explanation of the difference here, and reference grammars do not help. (Some ideas are presented in Yule (1986) on this difference and also on the examples of 'appropriate' utterances presented below.)

A second danger is that if the rule is probabilistic, but is stated as categorial, then the teacher is providing the learner with a solid basis for future confusion, or even error of the type referred to as 'induced error' by Stenson (1974). A good example of this is the common explanatory 'rule' that adjectives like *interested* or *bored* are used to describe people, whereas the forms *interesting* and *boring* are used to describe things. While this is certainly true, it is not the whole truth. If the learner applies the rule conscientiously, then he or she will be led to describe the teacher as *interested* when he means *interesting*. (Note that, in such a situation, the process does not necessarily lead to ungrammatical expression, but to the learner possibly being interpreted as meaning something other than intended.) This is one small example of the type of mistake some learners probably make because they have learned a rule and apply it too generally.

For many teachers, these potential dangers are not sufficient grounds for abandoning many of the traditional rules which can serve as useful supports for the learner in the earlier stages. It may indeed be a need of all those embarking on an attempt to acquire new skills that there be some strong regularities to grasp on to at first. (Young children, acquiring their first language, do seem to want to make the language highly regular in its form–function correspondences; they may, for example, add -*ed* to all verbs referring to past time, producing not only *walked*, but also *runned* and *drinked*.) However, there comes a point at which many language teachers realize that the 'support' created by the rule must be removed if the learners' needs for progress are to be met. This is a difficult transition, from one view of the language as a generally rigid, categorially organized and fairly restricted set of data, to an alternative view in which the language is a flexible, non-categorial, functionally oriented, and rich system of expression. For many teachers, that transition is something which will happen to their learners outside, not inside, the classroom. Yet, for other teachers, the whole aim of classroom instruction is to provide a sufficient sample of language experiences, in a supportive environment, to prepare the learner to take part in the language-using community outside the classroom.

The difficulties such teachers face are monumental, and we do not pretend to be able to provide some instant solution. What we hope to offer is *a set of techniques for looking at both language and the learner* which can equip the teacher to determine, more specifically, the sample language experiences which would be beneficial for a particular group of learners. In looking at language, we are not going to work from rules and explanations about it, but from a general concept that what language users make use of is 'communicative competence'. This, we believe, will provide a better perspective from which to consider aspects of the learner's needs.

Communicative competence

In recent years, there has been a major shift in perspective within the language teaching profession concerning the nature of what is to be taught. In relatively simple terms, there has been a change of emphasis from presenting language as a set of *forms* (grammatical, phonological, lexical) which have to be learned and practiced, to presenting language as a *functional system* which is used to fulfill a range of communicative purposes. This shift in emphasis has largely taken place as a result of fairly convincing arguments, mainly from ethnographers and others who study language in its context of use, that the ability to use a language should be described as *communicative competence*. Key components of communicative competence, as presented by Canale and Swain (1980), are grammatical competence, sociolinguistic competence, and strategic competence.

Given this description of the separate components, we can characterize traditional language teaching methods and materials as concentrating on the development of *grammatical competence*, almost to the exclusion of the other components. Thus, a syllabus or a textbook which presents the grammar, the lexicon, or the phonology of a language as a set of forms and rules to be learned should have the effect, if successful, of giving learners the ability to produce grammatically or phonologically accurate sentences in the language being studied. Developing this grammatical competence, it should be remembered, is in many respects the major goal of large numbers of students who take courses in a second or foreign language. Moreover, it has never really been seriously suggested that any language learner can become proficient in a language without developing a certain level of grammatical competence. We shall explore the role of grammatical competence in investigating learners' needs in Chapter 7.

Concentration on developing only grammatical competence, however, will not provide the learner with the ability to produce sentences or utterances which are appropriate to the context of use, or to interpret the appropriacy of such utterances. This ability, called *sociolinguistic competence*, allows the language user to select which utterance form, from any number of possible correct forms, is considered *appropriate* within a language community on a particular interactive occasion. Typical illustrative examples of this component might be the following two ways (in English) of getting someone to give you something:

6 Give me that knife!
7 Can I have that knife?

Both of these linguistic expressions are equally well-formed in grammatical terms, but part of an English speaker's knowledge of the language would involve a recognition that they would each convey different things, according to their context of use. Very generally, one would expect the first to be treated as a direct command and the second to be treated as an indirect request.

The treatment of language in terms of communicative functions, with requesting or commanding as simple examples, has become very common in commercial language teaching materials in recent years. Instead of grammatical items being presented, illustrated, and practiced, there are functional items. Instead of drills to practice the English present progressive, for example, there are drills which practice how to ask for permission. Many language teachers, enthusiastic about fostering sociolinguistic competence, have nevertheless become quite dissatisfied with material of this sort. In many ways the material often seems no different from a tourist's phrase-book. This is the unfortunate outcome of reducing the complex processes involved in the interactive use of language to a set of linguistic expressions to be learned, with the implication that a predictable relationship exists between each communicative function and specific linguistic expressions. We suspect that many language teachers react unfavorably to this type of material because it represents an extreme distortion of their experience as language users. When asked if some expression is appropriate or not, language teachers inevitably reply with some version of 'it depends on the context'. This is an intuitive recognition that communicative function cannot be isolated from sociocultural context and, consequently, that functional values cannot be assigned to linguistic expressions in isolation. Fostering sociolinguistic competence, then, must be tied to developing a sensitivity to linguistic variation within different social contexts. It is not enough to memorize thirty different phrases which may be used to 'express an opinion'; one needs to know the social conditions which would cause one of these expressions to be the most appropriate within a particular social context. The extent to which representative experiences of such contexts can be offered in language classrooms, and how the needs of language learners in this area can be identified, will be explored in Chapter 8.

The third major component of communicative competence is *strategic competence*: in simple terms, the ability to successfully 'get one's message across'. This is more typically a matter of effective transactional (rather than interactional) skills. The investigation of strategic competence is very much tied to the use of communication strategies which enable language users to organize their utterances as effectively as possible to get their messages across to particular listeners. Such strategies are also considered to be part of the ability to repair, or compensate for, breakdowns in communication. These 'strategic' aspects of the language user's overall competence have not received as much attention as the other two, yet they are clearly crucial elements in the second language learner's repertoire. While it is, in fact, a necessary part of all communicative interaction, the ability to organize and express one's message in a second language has a rather special urgency about it. Much of the work done in the investigation of communication strategies has concentrated on how learners cope with situations in which there is a gap between communicative intent and the expressive means available. For example, if learners simply do not know a vocabulary item, should they just fall silent and avoid trying to talk about that 'thing' they cannot refer to in the second language? Or should they find a way to get round this gap in their grammatical competence? It is our experience that few classroom learners are systematically provided with opportunities to develop their strategic competence in the second language, and we shall try, in Chapter 9, to illustrate the ways in which investigations in this area can benefit both teacher and learner.

Any genuine attempt to meet learners' needs in terms of communicative competence forces language teachers to take into account a great many factors not traditionally considered part of the language lesson. One obvious example is the importance of the interlocutor in consider-ations of both sociolinguistic and strategic competence. Producing *appropriate* utterances in a particular situation depends very much on the individual to whom those utterances are addressed, and the other individual(s) present during the interaction. Producing communicatively *successful* utterances also depends on making correct assumptions about what the interlocutor knows, or doesn't know, already. Yet, in the trad-itional classroom, the teacher is the only second language interlocutor most students encounter. The teacher's status is relatively fixed and his or her knowledge usually assumed to be substantial. As a consequence, major changes in the organization of classrooms and lessons (for example, more 'role play' and 'group work') tend to be necessary when the learners' communicative needs are addressed. Such changes are also an acknowledgment that substantial variation exists in the use of language, not only in relation to the interlocutor, but also in accordance with the type of topic or the nature of the communicative task. We shall return to these issues in Chapter 10.

These are all aspects of changes in the concept of the 'domain' of language teaching. This has broadened to include the domain of communicative interaction, which has many more dimensions than that of language seen as a static object under investigation. Yet, a larger domain does not necessarily lead to more successful language learning experiences for the learner. On the contrary, it holds an even greater potential for confusion and frustration. As a result, effective analysis of what the language learner needs in order to function within that domain has become more urgent, and the way in which that analysis is made requires careful scrutiny.

3   The analysis part

Needs analysis in education is typically carried out in very general terms. In such studies, a great deal of attention is devoted to considerations of demography, socioeconomic factors, educational history (both of institutions and individuals), the current structure of the educational system, and a number of other elements such as religion, or politics, or ideology, for example, which may be relevant to some particular pedagogical setting. However, throughout most of this book, we shall be concerned with the more narrowly focussed type of investigation which individual teachers can carry out, in the classroom, with their own particular groups of students.

In many ways, as we have tried to emphasize already, practicing language teachers frequently organize their teaching on the basis of some intuitive, informal analysis of the needs of their students. Yet, those teachers do not often feel that what they do, based on intuition, has much value beyond the daily workings of their classrooms. They probably suspect that some 'expert' would decide that their ideas were naïve, or that their methods were lacking in validity or reliability, or even that, according to published research, one of their cherished techniques is significantly less effective than some other new technique.

We would like to suggest that practicing teachers could put a little more faith in their own judgments, and defend them against so-called 'experts', if they could support those judgments with some research of their own. That research, we shall argue, can be carried out in classrooms, during class time, and can contribute to the learning experience of the students while yielding information which the teacher can use for analytic purposes, and which will also be of interest to other teachers in other classrooms. We think that it is very important that a research instrument should have the potential to be used as a teaching instrument and we have tried to design our materials with this in mind. Before we illustrate some of the practical research methods we have used for needs analysis, let us consider two issues which seem, unnecessarily, to have discouraged many language teachers from carrying out, or reporting on, their own investigations.

The inevitable numbers

Informally, most language teachers tend to talk to each other about their learners' language development in qualitative terms. They say that their students are, or are not, 'improving', 'becoming more fluent', 'writing a lot better', 'taking part more in group discussions', and so on. This seems appropriate, since few would deny that second language learning is a process in which qualitative change is the goal. Yet, perhaps paradoxically, the typical means employed to analyze such change is quantitative. Virtually every investigation of language learning produces numerical data in one form or another. The assumption, of course, is that qualitative change, or some key aspects thereof, can be described effectively in numerical terms. Among those who have questioned this assumption is Patton (1981), who points out that although quantitative methodology is a part of what he calls the 'dominant paradigm' in educational research, qualitative methodologies are also in existence, and in fact are often the methodologies which are most useful to the classroom teacher (as opposed to the educational researcher). The dominance of quantitative approaches, however, has produced a rather unfortunate effect in the domain of second language teaching.

If research yields numerical data and the interpretation of those data has to be carried out in statistical terms, then few language teachers consider themselves capable of undertaking such research. Since many of those who enter the language teaching profession are generally uncomfortable with the whole idea of 'doing statistics', they have not sought training in that area and consequently disqualify themselves, in their own eyes, from research activity in general and needs analysis research in particular. We suspect that, for many trainee language teachers, there exists a kind of 'statistics anxiety', analogous to the more frequently recognized 'math anxiety' experienced by many students in the social sciences and humanities. We also believe that, despite this anxiety, virtually all language teachers do in fact carry out statistical analysis, to some degree, as part of their work in the classroom. The problem, then, is essentially a matter of perspective on what 'doing statistics' means.

Let us try to exorcize one demon by describing it in basic terms. Statistics is simply a branch of mathematics which deals with the collection, analysis, and interpretation of numerical data. Under this definition, any language teacher who has administered a quiz to a group, counted the correct scores, worked out the average, and identified some students as having above-average scores or below-average scores has performed a statistical analysis. In essence, then, the use of statistics is simply a means of quantifying performance (for example, counting correct answers), typically via some objective measuring device (for example, the same quiz under the same conditions for everyone), which is considered relevant or valid for the particular type of performance under investigation (i.e. language skills and not needlepoint skills). One type of statistical analysis (for example, working out the mean, or arithmetical average, of a set of scores) deals primarily with the numbers, not with the content of the quiz. However, arguments over the validity, or the generalizability, of the designation 'above average' do relate to the content, and are also a statistical matter. If teachers wish to claim that performance on their quiz is a reflection of a student's general ability in *using the language*, then they will have to show that their quiz contains a representative sample of what is required in general use of the language. This can be done by showing that there is a high probability that ability to do x (for example, choose correct answers on the quiz) will consistently indicate ability to do y (for example, use the language generally). This is a specific version of a classic linear relationship utilized in psychometric investigations and stated most succinctly by Cronbach and Meehl (1955: 283–4) when discussing the crucial concept of construct validity: 'a construct is some postulated attribute of people assumed to be reflected in performance . . . persons who possess this attribute will, in situation x, act in manner y (with a stated probability).' Measures of statistical probability are consequently very important in the development of standardized proficiency tests such as TOEFL, since general claims about proficiency in the language as a whole are projected from performance on an extremely small sample of exam questions.

However, it is worth noting that few language teachers who might undertake needs analysis are interested in making such general claims about the outcome of their investigations—claims which require measures of statistical probability. Quite the opposite. They typically want to identify local needs among a very specific population—for example, their twenty students—who, by definition, are not a representative sample of all language learners. As Gaies (1983:196) has pointed out, teachers inevitably work with 'accidental sampling', or a sample which is conveniently at hand. Consequently, although there are highly sophisticated and extremely reliable statistical measures available for measuring general probability, they really do not serve the primary needs of most language teachers undertaking local research in their classrooms.

Most language teachers simply wish to elicit information on what *their* students need to know and know already. They can often do this relatively effectively using descriptive statistics—calculating, for instance, how often a learner uses a particular linguistic form in different contexts. Such a question can be answered in terms of quite simple numerical computations and expressed as percentages or other ratios. For the most part, these numerical data will simply represent answers to questions beginning 'How many … ' or 'How often … ' which the teacher can use to distinguish between different types of performance on different measures. What the teacher finds via those measures provides insight into what students can do, what they can't do, where they need some support, and so on. The teacher rarely wishes to use such information to make 'significant' claims about all language learners and so does not *need* measures of statistical significance. So, in fact, numbers are not the barrier preventing teachers from doing systematic and useful classroom research.

The real problem, for most classroom investigations, is designing effective research procedures so that the resulting numbers are a fair reflection of what learners are capable of. We have to emphasize this point. Investigations of learners' needs require good research procedures much more than they require sophisticated knowledge of statistics. In the following section we shall briefly discuss the research question issue, and throughout the whole book we shall illustrate and justify the value of different kinds of research procedures, yet we shall rarely appeal to any statistical operation which cannot be carried out using a standard pocket calculator. This is not a product of some anti-statistical bias. We firmly believe that those who wish to make global claims about the nature of language learning or acquisition, or to promote the value of one methodology or one set of materials over any others, should submit their claims to extremely rigorous testing to eliminate personal or ideological preferences and to produce valid and generalizable results. The statistical operations required are widely known and readily available in texts which relate specifically to the study of language (for example, Hatch and Farhady 1982; Butler 1985; Woods, Fletcher, and Hughes 1986).

Like most practicing language teachers, we have much more limited goals and operate at the opposite end of the spectrum. We would, ideally, prefer to know what each *individual* language learner needs in our classrooms. Yet, in practice, we simply do not have the time to carry out large numbers of case studies. We have to work at the group level and treat individuals as members of groups whose second language needs we can attempt to identify, tentatively, with an awareness that we may not always get it right. It is primarily a descriptive process which often has no specific well-formed hypothesis to test. Mostly it starts with a general idea or intuition about what is going on in the way a particular group of learners tries to cope with the experience of learning a second language. Our work is exploratory and may, if successful, give rise to hypotheses which can, in a future study, be tested under the rigorous conditions and with the kind of control of variables which few active language teachers can guarantee in their classroom work. We trust that, by example rather than by rhetoric, we can convince the 'statistically anxious' teacher that the collection of relatively simple numerical data from exercises conducted in classrooms does provide greater insight into learners' needs, and that working with the inevitable numbers is a quite familiar activity rather than an encounter with demons to be feared and avoided.

The research question

For many language teachers and teacher trainees, the term 'research' seems to conjure up work done in a laboratory setting by full-time investigators who devote considerable attention to controlling variables in their experimental designs and who publish highly technical reports containing tables of figures which indicate where statistically significant results have been obtained. While research of this type has indeed made an important contribution to the study of second language acquisition, it should not be treated as the only, or even the best, route to take in investigating the needs of language learners. Few practicing language teachers have the time, the facilities, or the training to satisfy the rigorous requirements imposed by the experimental sciences. There are also fundamental administrative and ethical problems involved. Very few language teaching programs will allow their students to be randomly assigned to different classes (to create the control versus the experimental group) for the purpose of investigating the effects of a particular method of instruction, for example. Moreover, there really does seem to be a difficulty, in the real world of language instruction, of establishing well-defined, objective constraints on the range of factors which have a potential influence on any individual's learning experience. In short, the language classroom is simply not a reasonable facsimile of the experimental laboratory.

However, this does not mean that language teachers are excluded from the research endeavor. If we can define any research activity as an attempt to carry out an investigation as thoroughly and systematically as possible in the prevailing circumstances, in order to provide information on a particular topic or to answer some predetermined question(s), then we shall find such activity, in one form or another, in any language teaching situation. The more narrowly defined the question that is asked, and the more controlled the methodology used to arrive at the answer, then the closer the teacher's research activity will come to that of the professional researcher. The more general the topic on which information is sought, and the more open the elicitation procedures used, then the greater the differences between the activities of teacher and experimenter will be. And, in fact, *all* second language acquisition researchers must make the choice between relatively narrow and wide focus; individual researchers seem to establish definite preferences in the type of focus they prefer.

This difference between narrow and wide focus should always be recognized as a trade-off situation. The more narrowly focussed the research instrument, the more clearly we should be able to see the small detail of an object under study, yet, in the process, we inevitably lose sight of all that surrounds the object. The more widely focussed the research instrument, the broader will be the view encompassed, yet, in that process, the more blurred will be the details of any particular object. The sensible conclusion, if we do not wish to sacrifice one type of view, is that there must be value in attempting to maintain both perspectives. In consequence, we have to recognize that there must be a range of research activities possible within the study of learners' needs and that, in different circumstances, some procedures will be more appropriate and more feasible than others.

We shall provide illustrations of these different types of procedures in the following chapters. Where we have been able to carry out an investigation to answer a very specific question with a narrowly focussed research instrument, then our report will include a lot of procedural detail, information on subjects, and quantified results. In such cases, we shall place great emphasis on making sure that our claims are consistent with, and limited to, our findings. Where our investigations have been based on a broader view and are much more exploratory in nature, we shall report on general features and tendencies and suggest possible directions in which further research should be undertaken before more specific claims can be made.

We suspect that it is this second, less narrowly focussed perspective which most practicing language teachers associate with 'doable' research in the classroom. We hope that we shall be able to encourage teachers not only to pursue investigations of this type, but also to think about ways to test their general conclusions by going on to design more narrowly focussed research procedures. We recognize, from experience, that language teachers tend to be interested in discovering, in an exploratory manner, what their own second language students can or cannot do in a particular situation. We usually find that there is an implicit comparison with the performance of native speakers in a comparable situation. We would like to persuade language teachers to make that comparison explicit, by illustrating the pedagogical advantages of collecting native speaker data.

For example, if we develop a simple classroom exercise in which ESL students are asked to describe some unfamiliar objects and we find that the students typically respond with expressions like *I don't know the name* or *I can't say what's this*, then we have certainly discovered something worth knowing about these students' performance in the language. If we then ask a number of native speakers to perform the same task and, instead of the 'I don't know' type of response, we hear expressions like *Well, it's like a kind of brush, I guess, with a handle at one end and something sticking out the other end*, then we have found not only a difference between these learners and native speakers, but a genuine example of the type of expression these learners might be encouraged to try to produce when they don't know what something is called. (We shall describe exercises of this type in greater detail in Chapter 9.) In such a situation, we have not explicitly formulated a specific hypothesis and have not controlled the experimental procedure. Nor did we intend to quantify the findings of the investigation and submit the figures to statistical analysis. Yet, we certainly have identified a specific phenomenon which we could go on to investigate more thoroughly and systematically. The first, and most important step, however, in terms of practical classroom research, is the discovery of an effective elicitation procedure which provides relevant language data with which to work. The important point here is that there are practical advantages to be derived from the type of investigation which is largely pre-theoretical and constrained by the 'doable' criteria imposed by the circumstances of a particular classroom. It is an example of what has been called 'action research', defined by Brumfit as 'research which is motivated by a specific local problem and is designed only to resolve that problem in that setting' (1984:143). In addition to those practical advantages, such an investigation can serve as a preliminary stage in the development of a more narrowly focussed research instrument which seeks to pinpoint just what specific communication needs some student, or group of students, may have.

In the course of this book, we shall place great emphasis on the importance of elicited data in the analysis of learners' needs. We have no hesitation in admitting that much of the research in this area is, at the moment, still at a descriptive, exploratory stage. We do believe, however, that such a stage is a necessary, but frequently omitted, aspect of basic research in the language teaching field. All too often, we present learners with unrealistic target behaviors, exemplified by materials in which 'ideal' native speakers unhesitatingly produce flawless sentences in generic situations. Such an approach was perhaps forgivable in an era when it was generally believed that the structural components of the language could be mastered, one at a time, via pattern-practice activities in which only good habits (i.e. flawless sentences) should be fostered. We have, however, entered a different era in which we wish to claim that we can provide learners with the means to accomplish things via the second language. Yet, we have only begun to explore just what is involved, in practical teaching terms, in implementing such a claim. We need to undertake basic research, at the classroom level, to discover what our learners intend to accomplish. We have to investigate the ways in which those learners go about accomplishing things (and how they fail to accomplish things) via the second language. We also have to discover how native speakers of a language go about accomplishing things in comparable situations. These are general statements of directions in which our research should go. Converting those statements into specific research questions that can be answered in a particular pedagogic setting is a process which will be exemplified over and over again in the chapters which follow.

Further reading

Easily accessible recent accounts of the range of methods and procedures in language teaching can be found in Bowen, Madsen, and Hilferty (1985), Larsen-Freeman (1986), Richard-Amato (1988), or Richards and Rodgers (1986). Krashen's views on the role of learning can be found in Krashen (1981, 1982, 1985) and in Krashen and Terrell (1983), with critical reviews and some counter-arguments presented in Gregg (1984, 1986), McLaughlin (1987), Scarcella and Perkins (1987), and Spolsky (1986). On the fossilization issue, which goes back to Selinker (1972), see the interesting discussion by Vigil and Oller (1976), or the work of Schumann (1978b). For an insightful discussion of learning purpose, see Widdowson (1983) and, for an account of some teachers' frustrations in this area, read Medgyes (1986). General discussion of classroom organization and activities to promote cooperative learning can be found in Kagan (1985). Eclecticism is the key to collections such as Oller and Richard-Amato (1983) and Celce-Murcia and McIntosh (1979). On issues related to pedagogical grammar, see Widdowson (1979, 1980) or the recent collection edited by Rutherford and Sharwood-Smith (1988). A strong argument against categorial rules is to be found in Givón (1979). A general introduction to English grammar for ESL teachers is provided by Celce-Murcia and Larsen-Freeman (1983) and on the concept of induced error, see Stenson (1974). The original arguments for the concept of communicative competence can be found in Hymes (1971), with Canale and Swain (1980) as a good overview of the language teaching issues. On needs analysis generally, see Buckingham (1981), Munby (1978), Richterich (1983), Richterich and Chancerel (1980), and Yalden (1987). For a valuable recent discussion of the uses of quantitative and qualitative approaches to second language research, and the relationship between these, see Wolfson (1986), Henning (1986), and Chaudron (1986), and on the relative merits of different introductory statistics texts, see Grotjahn (1988). Two recent volumes on second language research in classrooms are Chaudron (1988) and Seliger and Shohamy (in press).

PART TWO

What learners need to know

Introduction

The term 'needs analysis', when it has been used in the context of language instruction, has usually referred to the collection and evaluation of information to answer the question: 'What aspects of the language does some particular group of learners need to know?' It is impossible, for a variety of reasons, not the least of which is lack of time, to teach *all* of any language; some selection must take place. Mackey (1965:161) puts it this way: 'Selection is an inherent characteristic of all methods. Since it is impossible to teach the whole of a language, all methods must in some way or other, whether intentionally or not, select the part of it they intend to teach.' However, not all selection is particularly effective, according to Mackey.

> The great amount of material taught by some methods includes much that is never used and soon forgotten. A learner often memorizes as many as 12,000 words in order to be able to understand a particular 1,000. This is because there is no relationship between the wide selection made and the limited purposes of the learner. ... A person may have a most extensive vocabulary in the literary language and still not have enough to order a meal. The well-known French writer, André Gide, for example, who had such a wide knowledge of the English literary vocabulary, as shown by his excellent translations of Shakespeare and Conrad, was quite unable, according to his friend Julian Green, to ask a London bus driver where to get off.
> (loc. cit.)

Implicit in Mackey's statement is the assumption that language is variable, and that, within any given language, there exist *registers*, or language varieties which are conditioned by social context. Such registers may vary from one another in vocabulary; for example, the register of auto-mechanics may make common use of items like 'crankcase', 'piston', and 'spark-plug' which are extremely rare in other registers. While Mackey, as quoted above, seems to imply that registers differ only in terms of vocabulary, it is clear that they may also differ in terms of grammar. Research on Language for Special Purposes (LSP) has shown that registers differ in the frequency with which certain grammatical forms are used, and the function to which those forms are put. For example, such research has shown that the passive construction tends to be used with greater frequency in the register of scientific writing than in other registers of English (cf. George 1963; Cooray 1967; Swales 1976) and, as we shall see in Chapter 5, LSP researchers have also claimed that the passive/active distinction serves a function in scientific journal writing which is usually not described in English grammar books. If it is true that the specific items of vocabulary and grammar which must be mastered by a language learner are *register-specific*—that is, that such items vary in frequency when language is used in different contexts—there are definite implications for syllabus construction for the language classroom. In many cases it is possible that a learner like Gide, who is learning the language for a very specific purpose, needs, in the short run, to focus only upon the learning of a single register, and this only in the written mode. Of course, as Mackey's example also illustrates, Gide did encounter unforeseen needs for the language, namely the use of the oral register required for effective use of public transportation. However, it is often possible, to differing degrees, to limit the registers of the language which are taught, based upon an investigation of the identifiable aims of any group of learners.

Such an investigation may reveal serious gaps between the language syllabus and the students' needs for the language. What are language teachers to do when they realize that their students need to use the language in situations which their textbooks do not prepare them for, and even in situations in which the teachers themselves haven't functioned? For example, some ESL teachers in the United States, who have never entered a welfare office themselves, have had refugee students who needed to use English in the welfare office. Should these ESL teachers ignore their students' circumstances and just teach what is in the textbook? Or should they just make up a set of lesson plans based upon what they *think* happens in a welfare office? Or should they make some effort to gain first-hand information about this unfamiliar context, where their students have a pressing need for the language? Once teachers have decided that they want to know more precisely what language their students need in a given situation, they may choose among several courses of action, depending on the level of analysis they have energy or need for. They may ask their students to provide information of various kinds about the situation—for example, to bring forms from the welfare office to class, or answer a questionnaire about language needs in that context. Or such teachers may do some data gathering themselves; they may write a letter of enquiry, put in a telephone call, or set up an appointment and talk to native speakers who work in the welfare office. The most time-consuming method of gathering such data (and obviously the method most likely to provide the most accurate, detailed information on language use in the target situation) would be to get permission to tape-record oral interactions (either role-played or authentic) in the situation.

Obviously the course of action chosen will depend upon two things:

the amount of information needed for the particular class, and the energy level and interest of the teacher. A teacher who is committed to making some effort toward more direct needs analysis in the face of overwhelming student need, but who is overworked and underpaid, will probably have to settle for a more limited database. Nevertheless it is our belief that *any* effort made to gain accurate information about situations where our students need to use the language is a vast improvement over the alternatives of either ignoring that student need, or imagining that we can make up lesson plans based on what we suppose is needed in those situations.

Establishing what the learners need to know involves determining what the learners' aims are in learning the language (for example, getting a job as a sales clerk, or earning a BA in engineering), and then looking at the sorts of communicative behavior which native speakers of the target language (or, in a foreign language setting, fluent non-native speakers) engage in to achieve such aims (as, for example, understanding customers' questions and responding to them appropriately, or understanding lectures and taking notes). In other words, *the communicative behavior (real or hypothesized) of fluent speakers of the target language* is taken as a sort of measure by means of which we can establish what the learner needs to know about the language.

Of course, the process of establishing what a given group of learners needs to know, whether by intuitive means or by collecting and evaluating information of some kind, must surely go on long before language teachers ever step into their classrooms. It is carried out when the writer of a language textbook sets out to write the book, when the program administration sets up the program and the courses in it, when the curriculum committee decides on course goals and course content and chooses the textbooks. A great many individuals other than the language teacher are involved in the development of the curriculum for any language classroom, and of course, the topic of needs analysis at the program level has been treated very well in a great many books—books intended for program developers, program directors, curriculum committees, textbook writers and the like. Pehaps the most ambitious of these treatments is presented in Munby (1978), which takes the form of an extremely detailed model of an analysis of the communication needs of the language learner.

Such books typically focus upon what we would like to view as 'system-level' needs analysis: they suggest the collection and analysis of data on the linguistic and social context of the classroom; the characteristics of the educational system within which language instruction will take place; the attitudes of all participants toward the learning process itself; the career goals of typical students in the program, and so on. For example, Dubin and Olshtain (1986) suggest that the first step in designing programs and materials should be to identify the political and national context of the program, including patterns of language use in the society (i.e. the role of a language in the educational system and the labor market, and in furthering the process of modernization) and attitudes toward the language. Such information is of course essential to the planning of the curriculum for any language program, and many excellent books provide guidance for those interested in carrying out needs analysis on this system level. However, needs analysis only at the system level would focus upon the broad sociopolitical and educational context in which the learners will need to use the language—but would not provide specific information about the communicative behavior of fluent speakers. Strictly system-level needs analyses would not describe the three components of native speaker communicative ability (see below) with the degree of detail needed in order for the teacher to select precisely those aspects of the language which need to be taught.

Analysis in terms of communicative competence

If investigating what learners need to know involves some description of the communicative behavior of fluent speakers of the target language, then descriptions at the system level are not enough. In fact, we may (following Canale and Swain's 1980 description of communicative competence, which we have already discussed in Chapter 2) describe communicative behavior in terms of at least three interrelated dimensions.

Grammatical competence	Ability to produce and understand correct syntactic, lexical, and phonological forms in a language
Sociolinguistic competence	Ability to use a language appropriately in sociocultural contexts
Strategic competence	Ability to effectively transmit information to a listener, including the ability to use communication strategies to solve problems which arise in this process

Table 2.1   Three dimensions of communicative competence
(based on Canale and Swain 1980)

The dimension of grammatical competence entails the mastery of the grammatical, lexical, and phonological forms of the language; for example, native speakers of English know that *Please you can me help is an ungrammatical sentence. The dimension of sociolinguistic competence entails the ability to use the language appropriately in typical cultural contexts; so, native speakers know that it is inappropriate for a student to interrupt a university lecturer by shouting 'No, you're wrong!' The dimension of strategic competence entails the ability to effectively transmit information to particular addressees; referring to a

Scotch tape dispenser as an 'object roll' (as one of our ESL students did) would probably be viewed as an ineffective strategy by addressees who are native speakers of English.

An analysis of what a learner needs to know in the second language will usually reveal that the learner needs all three components of communicative competence. This will be particularly true if the learners are involved in a *second* language learning situation, as opposed to a *foreign* language learning situation—that is, if the learners are actually taking part in the culture where the second language is being spoken. In this case, they may encounter native speakers of the language outside the classroom in a variety of social situations, and will need to negotiate a wide variety of encounters in the second language. For this purpose, their language will need to be grammatical, appropriate, and effective.

In foreign language learning situations, however, their needs are likely to be narrower. A student may be learning English in Mexico solely for the purpose of reading journals in his or her field (see, for example, Mackay 1981), and may never intend to travel to an English-speaking country. Such a learner may feel very little need to develop oral skills or sociolinguistic competence in English. In this case, it may only be the learner's grammatical and strategic knowledge of the language in the reading mode which must be developed. But identifying precisely which aspects of communicative competence are needed, and therefore must be taught, requires that the investigator move beyond the system level of needs analysis and examine in detail the communicative behavior of fluent speakers of the language who read the sorts of material the learners wish to read.

Analysis from the 'inside' perspective

Many existing books on needs analysis are limited, as we see it, not only in that they take a system-level perspective, but also, and perhaps most crucially, in that they are written from the point of view of someone outside the classroom: this is often needs analysis done by and for outsiders. Hutchinson and Waters (1980) state the problem succinctly:

> There is a disquieting trend isolating needs analysis from other aspects of teaching and learning. The application of elaborate analysis models (e.g. Munby 1978) demands a curriculum 'expert', a creature apart from the teachers and learners ... the inevitable 'paper reality' takes its place—static, stereotyped, compartmentalised.
> (Hutchinson and Waters 1980:1)

While it is true that teachers may find the information provided by system-level 'expert' needs analysis to be useful, they are still the ones who must decide *how* to use this information. There are many decisions left to be made, decisions which cannot be made at the system level.

Classroom teachers, after all, are faced with actual individuals in a real place in real time, and they may find some discrepancies between the curriculum which has been given to them and the needs of their particular learners. Such discrepancies may arise because the decision-making procedure so beautifully outlined in books such as those mentioned above has not been followed very well—possibly an English language teacher in a country where teaching methods are very traditional has been given a textbook with a communicative syllabus, and finds that the students will not accept communicative methods and materials. More commonly, discrepancies may arise simply because of individual variation. While any general needs analysis may effectively establish the norm for a typical class within a particular social and educational system, in fact, every group of individual learners is different and may vary from that norm in unforeseen ways. For example, as we shall see below, Sorensen (1982) describes a situation in which she found, after teaching an ESL class for three weeks, that the textbook she had been assigned did not focus on the language skills needed *by that group of students*. It had always worked before with classes at that level—and in fact worked well in subsequent classes—but for a variety of reasons was inappropriate for *her* class. Sorensen had to re-analyze the communicative needs of those students while her class was in progress, and alter her course syllabus accordingly, in major ways. As we have argued in the Introduction to Section One, such a re-analysis and readjustment in response to the teacher's *ongoing* evaluation of what it is that the students need to learn is not at all uncommon and, while not usually as dramatic as that described by Sorensen, this process is in fact at the heart of all successful language instruction. (Increasing awareness of this type of evaluation is evidenced by the contributions in Alderson 1985).

Analysis of needs at four levels of generality

What we hope to do in this section is to describe ways in which teachers may more effectively carry out their investigation of what their students need to know about the language. In writing this description we have found that there is much to learn from the published literature on LSP. A familiarity with at least some of the findings in the published literature will, as we shall see, be helpful for teachers who need to make considerable readjustments to their syllabuses in response to their students' needs. And methods and instruments described in the published literature on LSP and needs analysis may easily be adapted for use by the classroom teacher.

It seems to us that needs analysis may be carried out—whether by a specialist or by a teacher—at any of four different levels: (1) the global; (2) the rhetorical; (3) the grammatical-rhetorical, and (4) the grammatical level. Such analyses may, of course, focus upon either written or spoken language at all four levels.

Level	Area specified	Examples
Global	The situations in which learners will need to use the language, and language-related activities which typically occur in those situations	In university classes: lecturing, taking notes, asking questions, reading blackboard notes
Rhetorical	The typical way information is organized in any language-related activity	In university lectures: an initial transition from yesterday's lecture, overview of points to be covered, review of standard procedure used in solving a problem
Grammatical-rhetorical	Those language forms used to realize the information structure of the language activity	(In the section of a lecture which reviews standard procedures) — use of the passive aspect as opposed to the active
Grammatical	The frequency with which language forms are used in different communication situations	(In engineering lectures) — the relative percentages of active and passive verb forms

Table 2.2   Investigating what students need to learn: four levels of analysis

The *global level* specifies the situations in which learners will need to use the language and the language-related activities required in those situations. At the global level, the basic question is, 'What do these students need to use the language for?' The aim, then, is to describe those types of communicative situations in which the learners will be using the language: where do the learners intend to use their second language, and what sorts of activities take place in those situations? Will the learners be waiting on tables, taking notes in engineering lecture halls, reading journal articles on veterinary medicine, reading technical manuals on the repair of engine parts, participating in class discussions? Or will they simply need to know enough of the language to pass a standardized test at the end of the term? Will they be required to transfer information from one mode to another, for example, from written prose to visual diagrams, or vice versa? (See Widdowson 1978 for a valuable discussion of 'information transfer').

Once the essential facts about the global level are known, one may then investigate the *rhetorical level*. The rhetorical level relates to the organization of information in the discourse which occurs within any given situation. Here one may ask 'How is information organized in the written texts encountered by the learner in the situations identified at the global level?' Another sort of approach which has recently been taken at the rhetorical level requires an analysis of the organization of an interaction in terms of functions. The subset of functions studied most is that of illocutionary function, or 'speech act'. Here, researchers might ask 'What language functions are required to be expressed or understood within communication situation *x*?' In waiting on tables, for example, do participants typically have to express an opinion, disagree, interrupt, summarize? Which of these speech acts occurs most frequently? Note that here we are asking about the communicative behavior of users of the target language—that is, we are asking what fluent speakers of the target language do within each of these situations in our attempt to establish what it is that *learners* of that language need to be able to do.

At the *grammatical-rhetorical level*, the goal of analysis is to determine what linguistic forms are used to realize the information structure established at the rhetorical level. For example, if one determines that journal articles in a particular field have a typical rhetorical organization, one may then ask, 'What language forms are used to signal that organization?' Perhaps it is verb tense or verb aspect that are used to signal the way information is typically organized and presented within such articles. If we are using the speech-act approach, once we have determined that fluent speakers frequently employ the function of 'expressing opinion' in academic discussions, we may go on to determine what linguistic forms are used by native speakers of the target language to realize that function. In practice, most researchers do not separate the rhetorical and the grammatical-rhetorical levels in their work. Most grammatical-rhetorical analyses are presented in two stages: first the rhetorical analysis, and second, the analysis of the way grammatical forms signal the rhetorical structure of the discourse.

Finally, the *grammatical level* relates to the frequency with which grammatical forms are used in specific communicative situations. At this level, we encounter a purely quantitative (as opposed to qualitative) form of analysis. Here the question is: 'What is the frequency of the grammatical forms used by fluent speakers of the target language in the set of communication situations identified in the analysis at the global level?' For example, how frequent is the simple present tense in newspapers? How frequent is it in academic writing? Is the passive voice used more in scientific writing than in everyday conversation? The answers to questions like these must be considered at the system level in selecting and sequencing points of instruction in different syllabuses: the passive might need to be taught sooner to science majors at the university than to tourists planning only to engage in informal conversations with speakers of the target language.

The outcome of such analyses at the grammatical level will of course be of interest to classroom teachers, as for example, when they find that their German class does not consist of science majors as they had expected, but rather contains mostly literature majors. But generally, for two reasons, classroom teachers will find it less feasible to carry out grammatical-level analyses themselves: first, such investigations typically require the statistical analysis of large bodies of data and are simply too time-consuming for the classroom teacher. And second, as we shall argue below, analyses at the formal level still leave the teacher with the problem of establishing *why* a particular form is more frequent in a particular register—that is, establishing what function that form plays in that register. This is a question which must surely be addressed in the course of teaching students to use the language accurately within the target situation.

In this section of the book, we will examine in more detail the global and grammatical-rhetorical types of analysis, as these seem to us to be most useful to, and doable by, classroom teachers. We will provide several examples of needs analysis which have been done at these levels by classroom teachers, teachers-in-training, and (occasionally) researchers. But we will focus primarily upon investigations carried out not at the system level, but rather at the level of a particular classroom as viewed from the perspective of the classroom teacher and a particular group of students.

4 Global needs analysis

A global needs analysis should identify the learners' purposes in learning the second language and arrive at a useful description of the situations in which the learners will need to use it, including in that description the types of language-related activities which typically occur in these situations. Will the learners be taking notes, reading directions, filling out forms, asking for information, taking orders, or leading discussions? What general language skills are required for these activities: grammatical, sociolinguistic, strategic? In what mode do they occur: reading, writing, speaking, listening?

Typical tools used in a global needs analysis are the questionnaire, the oral interview, and direct observation of both written materials and oral interactions central to communication in the target situation.

An example of such a global needs analysis carried out at the system level by a program developer is described in Mackay (1981). In designing an English program for Spanish-speaking students in the Faculty of Veterinary Medicine at the National Autonomous University of Mexico (UNAM), a structured interview was conducted using a field-tested questionnaire with professors and students at the university. Results indicated that undergraduates in veterinary medicine at UNAM needed English *only* in order to be able to read texts in their field of study. Oral skills and writing skills in English were not at all necessary for success in pursuing veterinary coursework at UNAM. While it is possible that some of these students would go on to use English in other contexts—in trips to the United States, for example—it was decided that only those language skills necessary for success at UNAM would be taught. A program was designed to meet these rather specialized needs.

While well-defined goals can often be established at the system level, often the learners in a particular language classroom may not have any very clear purpose for taking the language. For example, if a school system has a 'language requirement', students may simply be enrolled in a language class because they are required to be there. In such a case there may not be any external communicative situation within which they will need to use the language. Rather, their purpose may simply be (as we pointed out in Chapter 1) to pass the test at the end of the term. Nevertheless, even this much information will be of use to teachers. Knowing that their students will need to pass the test, and knowing that the students do not intend to use the language communicatively, teachers will be able to narrow the focus of what they will teach and the methodology they will use. So, for example, in this particular situation they may not want to use an oral communicative syllabus. This example, however, may be extreme. Usually students will have some plans— however remote and hypothetical—to use the language for some communicative purpose. And there is usually (though, we admit, not always) some system-level reason for 'language requirements'; for example, science majors in American universities may be required to study German because, it is argued, much valuable scientific information is available only in German documents. And usually we can identify situations in which the learners *will* have to make communicative use of the language.

A welfare case

As we have argued in the Introduction to Part Two, classroom teachers may need to investigate their own students' needs for the language. Let us consider a fairly typical case in which a teacher-executed needs analysis at the global level would be helpful.

Ms X is an ESL teacher of adult refugee students living in St Paul, Minnesota. She has been assigned a textbook organized along the lines of a situational syllabus: each chapter deals with a different social situation in which refugees typically need to use English: at the grocery store, on the city bus, at the post office, and so on. She is attempting to adapt the situational syllabus provided by her textbook by identifying those situations in which her particular students most need to use English communicatively. The simplest way to initiate this process is to give her students questionnaires. The teacher has, on the basis of questionnaires, identified ten such situations.

Almost all her students indicate that they need to visit the welfare office on a regular basis, and say that communication in the welfare office is important but problematic for them. However, this situation is not included in their textbook. Ms X, who has never been to a welfare office, realizes that she has no idea what sort of language (oral or written, productive or receptive) is needed in that context, or what sorts of speech events typically occur there. She can decide to ignore this need expressed by her students and simply select from among other situations in the textbook. Or she may decide to conduct some sort of investigation to find out more about language use in the welfare office. This investigation may involve giving a more specific questionnaire to her students to ascertain their perceptions; however, her students' perceptions may be inaccurate. She may therefore ask them to bring her samples of forms they need to fill out or other written materials from the welfare office. If she has time, her global needs analysis may also involve some direct contact with the welfare office itself: possibly interviews (by phone or face to face) with office staff, or even direct observation of interactions in the welfare office. The last option is obviously the most time-consuming, while also potentially the most informative. But *any* of the options suggested above would be helpful to this teacher.

Thus far, we have said that the goal of the global needs analysis is to establish the situations in which the target language will be needed, and the typical activities within those situations which require that language, either written or spoken. It is important here to make the point that, in most cases, some information usually needs to be gathered about the communicative situations identified. This is because teachers—even though they may be native speakers of the language—may not have first-hand experience of all the situations in which the language is needed. Even if they do have such first-hand experience, their memory of the communicative activities involved in those situations may not be accurate (since we are usually not analyzing the form of these activities when we are, for instance, buying stamps at the post office). Thus, the teacher cannot rely upon intuition or guesswork if the students' needs are to be accurately identified and the teaching materials are to be as useful as possible.

An agricultural case

Sorensen (1982) describes another classroom situation which required that the teacher do a global needs analysis. Sorensen was a graduate student and ESL teacher at the University of Minnesota, assigned to teach an English class to science students. For the first time since the course had been offered, it consisted primarily of students majoring in one area: agriculture. She had been assigned the usual textbook; however, she discovered, three weeks after the course had begun, that it was inappropriate: her students told her that it was not helping them in their classes, where they were having major problems with writing. A liberal arts major herself, Sorensen had no idea what language skills were considered important for students in agriculture classes, or what sorts of writing were typically required. While the textbook which was assigned focussed on writing, it contained primarily sentence-level grammar exercises, and required students to write only a few simple experimental descriptions. In this case, none of the work in the assigned textbook was difficult for the students—yet they complained that their writing skills were inadequate for the work they had to do in agriculture classes. Sorensen decided to do a global needs analysis which could meet a graduate course requirement while helping her teach her class more effectively.

The procedure Sorensen followed in conducting her global needs analysis was as follows. On the first day of class she had, as a matter of course, distributed a general sort of questionnaire to her students to gather information on their linguistic and academic backgrounds, the academic classes they were enrolled in at the university, and their purpose in studying English at the advanced level. When, in the third week of the course, a further needs analysis was conducted, Sorensen began by re-examining those questionnaires. She discovered that most of her students were enrolled in one or more of five courses, each representing a core requirement in the College of Agriculture. She decided to find out more about the writing requirements in those five courses. She interviewed the instructors in each of the courses, asking each for a copy of the course syllabus and discussing the course requirements with them, focussing specifically on the writing require-ments and the problems of their foreign students with these. When the writing requirements were compared, Sorensen found that they seemed to share in common the solution of a 'problem'. For example: 'Students in Field Crops are responsible for analyzing a given "problem", "collecting information and data" which they feel are needed "to tackle the problem", and for writing a report in which their "proposed solution to the problem is stated"' (Sorensen 1982:6). In the interviews, two instructors indicated that their foreign students had difficulty in 'posing' problems; in general the instructors indicated that the students had the most difficulty with the 'how and why' portions of 'problems', i.e. indicating 'how' they reached their solution, or 'why' certain factors were important. Sorensen observed that all these comments related to the students' difficulty in formulating a logical argument in their writing: without exception, the instructors agreed that, in performing these written exercises, logic was more important than grammatical correctness.

Sorensen then decided to examine a small sample of student papers which had already been corrected by these instructors, to see whether in fact the instructors' corrections and marginal comments focussed upon effectiveness in communicating information rather than on grammatical correctness: that is, in our terms, were the instructors more disturbed by their students' lack of strategic competence or grammatical competence in English?

This sort of data, rarely used by language teachers, seems to us to be extremely valuable when needs analysis is done within an academic context; that is, what do the learners' subject-matter teachers find problematic enough to comment on and 'grade down' on? Sorensen's conclusions may be somewhat surprising to some ESL teachers:

> ... the comments which the instructor made on the students' work generally did not occur where grammatical errors occurred, but were related principally to information gaps in the students' presentation of their arguments. The questions and comments which the instructor

wrote on the non-native speakers' papers were generally concerned with three main problems:

(1) the mentioning of a fact without showing how it applied to the given situation;
(2) the ignoring of facts which did not fit into a convenient generalization; and
(3) the elimination of a class of factors as possible disease agents because of the characteristics of a particular member of the class. (Sorensen 1982:10)

Sorensen concluded, as a result of her global needs analysis, that her students were having difficulty with writing assignments in agriculture courses not because of their problems with English grammar but because of their inability to set forth a logical argument in writing 'problem-solution' papers—specifically, their failure to express relationships between facts and to form accurate generalizations.

On the basis of this needs analysis it became clear why her textbook, which focussed almost exclusively upon sentence-level grammatical correctness, was inadequate. It contained *no* writing activities of the 'problem-solution' type, which might develop the learners' strategic competence, or more specifically, their ability to present clear argumentation in support of a conclusion.

Unfortunately, no other more appropriate textbooks could be ordered in time to be of use to the students. However, Sorensen *was* able to adjust the course syllabus and begin designing writing activities which provided practice in selecting and organizing data, posing problems, and drawing conclusions. Her global needs analysis was successful in helping her to produce writing activities of the problem-solution type, which were far more interesting and helpful to her students than those she had started out with.

Sorensen's needs analysis illustrates the importance of gathering real-world information in the actual situations in which students will be using the language. It is too easy for language teachers to *assume* that, for example, grammatical correctness is essential to student success in writing course papers at the university. This assumption may be unwarranted, and requiring students to spend long hours doing exercises which focus on grammatical correctness may not be particularly useful. In this case, it seems clear that the ability to organize information and present a logical argument in writing was far more important to the students' success in university agriculture classes than the ability to write grammatically correct sentences in English. Evidence is now accumulating to suggest that this sort of 'higher-level' communicative skill may be lacking for ESL students (and possibly for native speakers too) in other university fields as well.

An engineering case

When studying at universities in the United States, a great number of international students choose to major in engineering. They take ESL courses to prepare themselves to do well in courses in this field. Yet most ESL teachers have a liberal arts background and have no first-hand knowledge of what sorts of communicative skills are used by engineering students at American universities. Jacobson (1987), a graduate student and ESL teacher at the University of Minnesota, undertook to study the communicative skills used in one of the course sequences required for all undergraduate engineering students, a general physics laboratory. He gathered data using two methods: (1) interviews with the learners and the native speakers they worked with in the lab, and (2) direct observation (and audiotaping) of the learners' interactions with native speakers in the lab. These data were then analyzed in terms of communication problems which seemed to interfere with the learners' ability to complete their lab work successfully. Jacobson concluded that the learners' problems could not be pinned down to difficulties with grammatical forms of English *per se*, or even to difficulties with any particular mode (such as reading or listening). Rather, theirs was a problem with organizing information. Like Sorensen's agriculture students, these engineering students were having difficulty with higher-order skills—in this case, with evaluating, selecting, and synthesizing information in order to solve problems. Jacobson argues that much of this difficulty was language-related, involving, for example, the ability to distinguish given (or 'assumed to be known') from new information in lectures and readings, or the ability to use English in synthesizing information obtained from more than one source into a single conceptual framework. The suggestion that ESL students need more than traditional grammar work—that higher-order communicative skills are also needed by these students—should lead classroom teachers to re-evaluate the goals of their classwork. Many ESL textbooks may simply not be providing students with the opportunities to learn the communicative skills they need for such purposes.

Involving the learners

Appealing as the studies by Sorensen and Jacobson may be, most full-time language instructors may simply not have the time to carry out similar sorts of first-hand investigations: to investigate the behavior of native speakers in all the contexts in which their students participate, to interview their students' academic instructors or employers, and so on. We would like to suggest that, in fact, language teachers do not always have to personally gather data at the global level. Rather, the learners themselves may be able to provide valuable information on the sorts of communicative purposes for which they will be needing the language, particularly when they are learning the language in the culture in which it is used as a medium of communication. Indeed, Hanges (1982) points out that there are sound educational and philosophical reasons for having students tell the teacher what they need to learn; she cites Freire (1970) and Jenks (1981) in arguing that learners should be involved as much as possible in the development of their own instruction. She makes a point which we have made elsewhere in this book: that a learner-centred approach is to be desired, and that learners themselves can, with guidance, provide valuable information about those situations in which they need to use the language.

Hanges had been asked to teach a new course at the University of Minnesota, an advanced course in writing and research skills for graduate students. While she felt that she had a fairly clear understanding of what the research skills needs of her students would be, Hanges decided that her students would be responsible for identifying their writing needs in the academic programs they were about to enter. She would ask them to draw upon their own experiences and on information that they would collect in interviews with professors and other graduate students in their field. She gave her students a writing assignment which required them to conduct research into the nature of their *own* needs for written English in their chosen field. All the students were sent out to gather information within a common framework, a framework which they had all previously agreed to. They then reported the results of their research in writing to the teacher and the class. The assignment which they were given, a suggested outline for a written report, and a sample student report, are reproduced in Appendix 1. The data provided in these reports contained information at the global level regarding the kinds of writing assigned in required courses in their field, the amount of each kind of writing required, and examples of writing assignments (and even style guides) typically used in the courses concerned. On the basis of three academic quarters' worth of such student research, Hanges was able to devise writing materials which were of general use to graduate students in a wide variety of different fields.

Such global analyses provided *by the learner* create a number of advantages for the language teacher: they save the teacher a tremendous amount of time; they permit the learners to become the 'experts' on their own language learning needs and, through this involvement, to improve their motivation for language learning; they provide the teacher with access to primary data which might otherwise be hard to get (for example, quizzes and corrected pieces of student writing), and they allow for unexpected insights. So, for instance, a student may provide information about the use of English in an academic situation which the ESL teacher has not considered before, and would not have included in a teacher-made questionnaire. In Appendix 1, for example, the sample student report includes data on the average length of different kinds of papers required in Civil Engineering—information not requested by the teacher, but possibly valuable nevertheless. There are, of course, disadvantages to student-executed needs analyses as well. One of these is the possibility that individual students may not be accurate in their self-reports. Hopefully, as more and more data accumulate from more and more student-executed global needs analyses, such inaccuracies will become apparent. Certainly, at the global level, the student-executed needs analysis makes the most sense to the overworked language teacher who is unable personally to gather data in a wide variety of social situations outside the language classroom. Most learners are perfectly capable, with guidance, of providing this information on global-level needs themselves.

Student-executed needs analysis may even be useful in gathering data at other levels; for example, on actual language use in the 'real' world outside the language classroom. This possibility will be considered later, following Heath (1986), who suggests that learners can collect tape-recorded language data in target contexts and bring these to class for consideration. Learners can gather data on their own communicative performance, as we suggest in Chapter 8, or they can help to obtain data on the communicative performance of native speakers in those same contexts. It is to this last topic, the language used by native speakers in the social situations identified as important by the global needs analysis, that we now turn.

5 Grammatical–rhetorical needs analysis

1 Form and function in native speaker performance

In setting out what learners need to learn, we must move beyond the global level to a description of the language which is used by fluent speakers in the various situations which we have identified. In this chapter, we will examine some of the approaches which have been used at the grammatical–rhetorical level of analysis. It is important to stress again that we are here considering research on the way in which *fluent speakers* organize their communication in particular social contexts, together with the linguistic forms used by those speakers to realize that organization. Much of the recent research in this area on Language for Special Purposes (LSP) and English for Special Purposes (ESP) (see Further Reading for references) has examined the organization of communication in terms of speech acts and the linguistic forms used to realize these. In Chapter 8, we shall consider means of evaluating the abilities of second language learners with regard to the use of speech acts in the second language.

For special purposes: written language

For readers unfamiliar with the ESP literature, and the grammatical–rhetorical approach, we will briefly summarize developments in this field. Some of the earliest research on LSP set out to demonstrate that in language which *is* used for different purposes, grammatical forms may occur with differing frequency. At what we have called the grammatical level, some researchers counted the number of grammatical forms which occurred in chunks of language used for various purposes. So, for example, it was argued (by, among others, Swales 1976) that the English used in scientific writing contained a higher ratio of passive verb forms than the English used in popular magazines. Further, 'scientific English' could be characterized as containing more complex noun phrases, more nominalizations, and so on.

However, researchers in the 'grammatical–rhetorical' tradition (for example, Lackstrom, Selinker, and Trimble 1972) argued that this focus upon grammatical forms alone, while it provided a useful point at which to begin study, could not explain *why* speakers and writers had made the grammatical choices they had. Why did scientific writers (apparently) use the passive more? What leads the text-creator to use particular grammatical forms more frequently? Researchers, it was argued, had to establish the rhetorical structure of the text and its functions, and then relate grammatical choices to those functions. Beginning with 'The Washington School', represented most prominently by Louis Trimble and Larry Selinker, researchers began to try to establish typical structures of discourse within a particular genre and field, and then to identify the way in which these were related to grammatical choices made by the writer. (Widdowson (1981) described this approach as 'textualization'.)

So, for example, several researchers described the typical rhetorical structure of technical journal articles, and then attempted to show how the writer's choice of verb tense was related to that structure. For example, in a typical technical journal article, there is a section called 'reporting past literature'. Lackstrom, Selinker, and Trimble (1972) claimed that, in 'reporting of past literature' in a technical journal paper, writers seemed to use the present tense when claiming generality for the results reported in a study, and the past tense when claiming non-generality. That is, someone writing a technical journal article could choose to cite the same study results in two different ways, depending on his or her own point of view:

1 Smoking *causes* cancer (Smith 1980).
2 Smoking *caused* cancer in Smith (1980).

In example (1) above, the present tense is used because the writer wants to present Smith's findings as a 'general truth', i.e. smoking causes cancer. In (2), on the other hand, the writer uses the past tense in order to present the results as more limited in scope: smoking caused cancer in one study, but (by implication) might not cause cancer in other studies. Oster (1981) went even further, arguing that technical writers use the present tense when reporting research results congruent with their own views, and use the past tense when reporting research results not congruent with their own work. So, in simple terms, if technical writers agree with the results of a study, they are more likely to use the present tense in reporting it; if they disagree with those results, they are more likely to use the past tense.

Researchers in the grammatical–rhetorical school pointed out that students learning English in order to be able to read and write technical journal articles might not be prepared in their study of English grammar for this sort of grammatical–rhetorical relationship. Grammar textbooks available to learners in 1981 might, rather, lead them to expect that tense choice is made solely in relation to time—not in relation to the level of generality or the truth value of the content being reported. Grammar books might encourage such erroneous expectations, these researchers argued, because the rules for tense usage which were presented were not usually based upon an analysis of actual language use in particular fields and genres.

Another example of language in the grammatical–rhetorical tradition is Tarone, Dwyer, Gillette, and Icke (1981). This study looked at the use of passive verbs in scientific writing. As we have already pointed out, studies at the grammatical level had established that the passive was used more frequently in scientific writing than in other genres of writing. Tarone *et al.* asked what, in the rhetorical structure of scientific journal papers, might correlate with the choice of the passive over the active voice. Papers in astrophysics journals were chosen for study (although the same approach could as easily have been used with texts in any scientific field). An examination of papers in astrophysics journals showed, first, that the passive voice was used much less frequently than in other scientific writing. The rhetorical structure of papers in this field turned out to be different from that found in other scientific fields where more experimentation takes place, and this rhetorical structure in turn seemed to be related to the sort of non-experimental research done in astrophysics. One cannot experiment on a star the way one can experiment on an organic compound or a toad. So, papers in astrophysics do not report on experiments and their results; they are not organized in the 'typical' experimental format. Rather, they are shaped as logical arguments in which certain assumptions (or even assertions) are made by the writer, and certain logical consequences follow. Tarone *et al.* found that, at those points where astrophysics writers stated their assumptions, they used active verbs; at those points where they outlined the logical consequences which followed, they used passive verbs. Thus, grammatical choices (in this case, between active and passive voice) were made in relation to the rhetorical structure of the journal paper. One could not explain *why* active or passive voice was used unless one understood the rhetorical structure of this particular type of paper.

Both the studies in the grammatical–rhetorical tradition reported above focussed upon written language. How might the grammatical–rhetorical approach be used in the context of spoken language?

For special purposes: spoken language

At the outset, we would like to consider two studies which demonstrate grammatical–rhetorical analysis at the classroom level. These studies used a similar approach, and produced similar findings: further, they used a methodology which is adaptable to the needs of classroom teachers trying to work with and adapt the 'speech act' approach, so we describe them here in some detail. Both these studies required some analysis of the spoken language, as used by native speakers.

Burkhalter (1986), was teaching oral discussion skills in an advanced level ESL speaking class at an American university. In an initial examination of eleven ESL textbooks teaching discussion skills, she found five that presented language needed in discussions. The five texts taught very different sets of 'functions', and even where the same 'functions' were taught, the texts did not agree on the linguistic formulas used to realize them. For example, in four textbooks which presented the function of 'expressing an opinion' in oral discussions, Burkhalter found little agreement about which phrases to use. Out of a total of fifty-six different phrases taught as appropriate for this function by these four textbooks, only *five* were taught by more than one author, and only *one* was taught by all four textbooks (see Table 2.3).

Phrase	Book 1	Book 2	Book 3	Book 4
'As I see it . . .'	X	X	X	
'I believe . . .'		X	X	
'I think . . .'	X	X	X	X
'In my opinion . . .'		X	X	
'It seems to me that . . .'			X	X

Table 2.3   ESL opinion phrases taught by more than one textbook (Burkhalter 1986)

Burkhalter points out that since none of the ESL textbooks studied had cited research as the source of their taxonomies, it could be assumed that the authors had all relied on their intuitions as native speakers in setting out the linguistic expression to be used in realizing functions like 'expressing an opinion'.

Burkhalter decided to gather some speech data of her own to determine how accurate these authors' intuitions had been. She examined a forty-five-minute videotape recording of a group of native speakers of English conducting a discussion in an American university. She attempted to identify those points in the discussion where participants expressed an opinion, and her paper contains a very interesting discussion of the difficulty she (and various consultants) had in identifying when opinion-giving occurred. After reaching the best possible resolution of this point, she went on to tabulate the linguistic expressions which had been used to 'express an opinion'. She found that, of the fifty-six different linguistic expressions presented in these books as appropriate for the expression of opinion, only *three* were actually used by these native speakers to express an opinion in their discussion: 'Don't you think ...' (used 3 times); 'I'm pretty sure' (used once), and 'I think' (used 26 times). The phrase 'I think' was by far the most frequent expression used by these native speakers. Variants of other phrases taught in the ESL textbooks also occurred in the native speakers' discussions, but the exact phrases presented in the texts did not occur.

Williams (1988), in an EFL setting, uses a similar methodology to that employed by Burkhalter to investigate the language used by fluent speakers of English in business meetings in Hong Kong, and to compare it to the language taught by EFL textbooks in Hong Kong for business meetings. Interestingly, her study produced very similar findings to those of Burkhalter's, even in this quite different social and political setting.

Like Burkhalter, Williams first collected a set of EFL textbooks and listed the functions and linguistic structures presented by these books as being useful in business meetings. She then tape-recorded three business meetings (of about one hour each) which took place in Hong Kong, and transcribed the conversations so that she could analyze them in terms of functions. She compared the language used by fluent speakers in the business meetings with the language presented in the EFL textbooks, in terms of the functions which occurred and the linguistic expressions used to realize particular functions. She found, first, that there was little agreement among the textbooks as to which functions to teach for meetings. And, of the seventeen functions taught in these books for meetings, only ten in fact occurred in the business meetings observed. Further, out of a total of 135 linguistic expressions taught by the textbooks to realize the various functions presented, only seven were in fact used in the business meetings in three hours of talk (see Table 2.4). Williams points out that the functions used in the meetings were not necessarily realized explicitly, and often were realized by an extremely wide range of types of linguistic expressions (*not* taught in the EFL textbooks). She suggests that the EFL textbooks may not only be teaching students an inaccurate (non-native) set of expressions, they may also be teaching learners to be over-explicit in encoding their messages. (See Chapter 9 below for a discussion of learners' already-existing tendencies in this direction).

Function	Exponent	Number of times used
Disagree	'I'm not convinced that . . .'	2
	'Wouldn't it be better to . . .'	1
Express opinion	'I think . . .'	11
State intention	'I'll . . .'	3
Explain	'I mean . . .'	5
	'You see . . .'	3
Elicit	(interrogatives)	22

Table 2.4 Linguistic expressions used in business meetings (Williams 1988)

The classroom teacher will not usually have the time to gather hours of data on fluent speakers' oral communications in some target situation and to transcribe and analyze them in the detail reported here. However, it does seem reasonable to suppose that teachers might be able to adapt this procedure to their own circumstances. For example, teachers might be able to gain access to at least some native speaker communications and tape-record these in order to simply listen to them and gain an impression of the degree to which these communications approximate those delineated in a language text being used. Such recordings would be very useful in classwork as well, providing authentic texts for student study. Learners could be asked to listen to them and analyze, first, what sorts of speech acts these native speakers are performing, and second, what linguistic forms they are using to accomplish their purposes. Such a procedure would provide an interesting check on the claims implied by the text. Such a technique, we feel, fits in well with a learner-centered, problem-oriented pedagogical approach (described in more detail in Chapter 8 below).

Lest we have given the impression that it is only among 'functional' texts that inaccurate information about the use of the English language is presented, we should note that even among ESL grammar texts, where the emphasis is predominantly on the correct 'forms' of the language, there can be discrepancies. The existence of such discrepancies may in fact be one source of misinformation which many ESL learners bring with them from previous learning experiences. If, for example, the learners have been taught (via their textbook) that the English verb *try* must be followed by the infinitive (for example, *to go*) and have carried out reinforcing oral drills and written exercises, then they may be quite unwilling to accept (or at least be confused by) a new text which presents *try* with gerunds (as in *try reading more quickly*). Resolving this type of problem, as yet another example of what the learner needs to know, may ultimately only be possible by drawing the learner's attention to what native speakers actually do say and write in samples of naturally-occurring text.

Returning to our main consideration of the grammatical–rhetorical level of needs analysis, we have discussed the communicative behavior of fluent speakers of the target language in various genres and modes as if it were always both correct and homogeneous. That is, we have acted as if *all* fluent speakers always use fairly similar linguistic structures when they attempt to realize their communicative purposes in speech and writing. However, they do not. And, there are good reasons for pointing out this lack of consistency to language learners, as we shall argue in the next section.

2 Inherent variability in native speaker performance

Among many second language learners there seems to be a tendency to assume that all native speakers employ some uniform and fixed system of expression in their use of the language. This is often accompanied by a belief that native speakers have complete command of the 'whole' language or, in more specific terms, have all the vocabulary of the language at their fingertips. It is difficult to know where these assumptions come from. They may be fostered by the perfect sentences produced by characters in textbooks, or by the complete mastery evinced by their native-speaking teacher, or perhaps by the premium placed on uniquely correct forms required in answer to questions on typical proficiency tests. Whatever the cause, one drawback of such assumptions is that learners may perceive the task of self-expression in the second language as one requiring uniquely correct forms and structures. In other words, the learners may believe that there is one correct way to express an idea in the second language and, until they learn 'it', they will only commit errors. To avoid such errors, many learners simply keep quiet, possibly trusting that the transition from perfect silence to perfect proficiency will eventually occur.

We had suspected that non-conscious learner assumptions of this sort were involved to some degree in the classroom performance of some ESL learners, particularly those from China, Japan, and Korea. Recent informal discussions with advanced learners from these countries have confirmed that they had been extremely reluctant, during most of their English language training, to say anything unless they were sure that they knew exactly the right words and phrases. That such an approach to the learning and use of a second language may result from training procedures in their native countries, or may preserve powerful cultural constraints on how individuals should present themselves in public, are important points to recognize, and constitute an influence on some learners' performance over which we may have very little control. Yet, if the learner's approach is partially based on a misconception of how language is used, then we may be able to provide illustrations of the non-uniqueness of forms used by native speakers as a way of removing the misconception. To gather such illustrations is simply an exercise in documenting the variety of linguistic forms which native language users employ in accomplishing communicative acts. We could, in fact, use data from a number of other elicitation procedures described in other sections of this book to show learners examples of native-speaker variety in the spoken mode. However, since the written mode is normally considered to exhibit less variation, let us use a written exercise to make the point even more forcefully.

Eyewitness accounts

Fifty undergraduates enrolled in an introductory level lecture course at the University of Minnesota, all native speakers of American English, in the age range of nineteen to twenty-four years, voluntarily took part in the exercise. They were each given a copy of a cartoon-strip story, consisting of four pictures numbered one to four, shown in Appendix 2. They were also given a sheet of paper with the following instructions at the top:

'On the accompanying page there is a set of four drawings numbered 1 to 4, showing a series of events. Look over the drawings and work out what happened. Then, in the space below, describe briefly what happened, as if you had been *a witness* to the events and had to provide *an account for someone who had not seen what happened.*'

The subjects were asked if they had any questions and then instructed to begin writing. No time limit was imposed, but all fifty subjects finished the exercise within ten minutes.

When the written accounts were examined, it was found that no two accounts were identical. In an attempt to illustrate the similarity/variation of expression used, we have included a fairly large sample of part of our analyzed data in Table 2.5. The method of analysis follows procedures described in detail in Chapter 5 of Brown *et al.* (1984). Essentially, the set of events is treated as a series of actions involving characters, objects, and locations, which are linked to other actions by connectors. The linguistic expressions used by subjects to refer to those actions, characters, objects, locations, and connectors can then be identified and listed, in sequence, as in Table 2.5. The frequency of each expression used to describe a character, an action, etc. is simply displayed as a number out of fifty (i.e. the number of versions of the story elicited).

Referents	Linguistic expressions		Frequency/50
	Grammatical forms	**Examples**	
Character 1	Noun phrase	'a woman'	21
		'a lady'	20
		Name ('Mrs Smith')	9
Action 1	Verb	'was shopping'	33
		'went'	9
	Ø	—	5
		'was'	2
		'was walking'	1
Location 1	Prepositional phrase	'in the grocery store'	20
		'in the deli/delicatessen'	8
		'in the supermarket'	3
		Name ('in the Red Owl store')	3
	Ø	—	16
Connector	Conjunction/ New sentence		18
		'when'	13
		'and'	9
		'where'	1
	Ø	—	9
Character 1	Noun phrase	'she'	37
	Ø	—	13
Action 2	Verb	'met'	17
		'stopped to talk to'	11
		'ran into'	9
		'saw'	5
		'bumped into'	2

Table 2.5 continued

Referents	Linguistic expressions		Frequency/50
	Grammatical forms	**Examples**	
(Action 2)	(Verb)	'ran across'	1
		'came across'	1
		'spotted'	1
		'noticed'	1
		'recognized'	1
		'encountered'	1
Character 2	Noun phrase	'another woman/lady'	25
		'a friend/neighbor'	22
		Name ('Mrs Olsen')	3
Connector	Preposition	'with'	23
	Conjunction	'and'	14
	Ø	—	13
Character 3	Noun phrase	'her daughter'	15
		'her child'	13
		'her little girl'	9
	Ø	—	13
Connector	Conjunction/	'while'	24
	New sentence	'as'	9
	Ø	—	17
Characters 1 and 2	Noun phrase	'they'	22
		'the two (women/ladies)'	22
	Ø	—	6
Action 3	Verb	'were talking'	32
		'conversed'	5
		'were chatting'	4
		'were wrapped up in conversation'	3
		'were speaking'	1
		'caught up on gossip'	1
	Ø	—	4
Character 3	Noun phrase	'the child'	19
		'the girl'	18
		'the daughter'	13
Action 4	Verb	'took'	19
		'grabbed'	10
		'picked up'	9
		'removed'	2
		'pulled'	1
		'reached for'	1
	Ø	—	8
Object 1	Noun phrase	'a bottle'	39
		'a container'	1
		'an item'	1
		'a jar'	1
	Ø	—	8
Location 2	Preposition	'from'	15
		'off'	14
		'of'	3
		'off of'	2
		'on'	1
	Ø	—	15

Referents	Linguistic expressions		Frequency/50
	Grammatical forms	**Examples**	
(Location 2)	Noun phrase	'the shelf'	28
		'a shelf'	6
		'the counter'	1
	Ø	—	15
Connector	Conjunction	'and'	34
		'then'	4
	New sentence		4
	Ø	—	8
Action 5	Verb	'put'	30
		'placed'	8
		'slipped'	6
		'hid'	2
		'stuck'	2
		'deposited'	1
		'stuffed'	1
Object 1	Noun phrase	'it'	36
		'the bottle'	6
		'a bottle'	8
Location 3	Preposition	'in'	26
		'into'	24
	Noun phrase	'the woman's/lady's purse'	46
		'the purse of the woman/lady'	4

Table 2.5   Eyewitness accounts

The most obvious point to be made about the data presented in Table 2.5 is that there simply isn't one uniquely correct version of the story. As the table shows, in terms of vocabulary there is a greater range of expressions used when actions are described (i.e., verbs) than when characters are mentioned (i.e., noun phrases). The advantage of eliciting data from a fairly large number of subjects is shown in both the range of expressions elicited, for example, for Action 2 (*met, stopped to talk,* etc.), and also in the frequency count which indicates which expression (i.e. in Action 2, *met*) is the most commonly used. In addition to lexical variety, we also have evidence of choices made by subjects regarding how much information is to be included. Almost a third of the subjects omitted any mention of Location 2 (i.e., where the bottle was taken from). Note also that almost a third of the subjects did not include any specific mention of where the set of events took place (i.e., Location 1). This latter omission tends to coincide with the use of the verb *was shopping* to describe the first Action, thereby leaving the reader to infer the most likely location. Thus, we have a type of functional equivalence, despite differences in the forms and structures used, among the following set:

1 *A woman was shopping when she met a friend.*
2 *A lady was shopping in the grocery store when she stopped to talk to another woman and her child.*

3 *Mrs Smith was in the deli when she ran into a neighbor with her little girl.*
4 *A lady was in the supermarket. She met a friend with her daughter.*

Variation in the amount of explicit information included in an account can have an effect on how much interpretive work the reader has to do to follow the narrative. The more relevant detail included, the easier the reader's task should be in reconstructing the series of events, but there does seem to be some convention of avoiding extraneous detail. No subjects, for example, described what the characters were wearing. There may also be a convention of avoiding insufficient detail, though this may be harder to define. Some subjects (13 out of 50) chose not to introduce the little girl into the narrative when they introduced the second female. Consequently, in those subjects' accounts, the little girl suddenly appears later as a new character (though always identified by the definite article *the*, as if already known) who performs Action 4. In such accounts, the reader may not have an accurate picture of where this little girl came from. From such observations, we may conclude that there is possibly some basic, or desirable, level of explicitness in written accounts of this type, though substantial variation from this basic level will be encountered. One way to arrive at a possible model for the basic level, involving the most common lexis, would be to construct a version of the narrative which employs the highest frequency forms in each category listed in Table 2.5. That version would read as follows:

A woman was shopping in the grocery store. She met another lady with her daughter. While they were talking the child took a bottle from the shelf and put it in the woman's purse.

None of our fifty subjects actually produced this account. It is a constructed 'skeleton' account from which any actual account will inevitably vary. It represents, then, a basic format from which type and quantity of variation can be analyzed. In the language teaching situation, it should allow teachers to compare typical native speaker variants with those produced by a group of learners. It should also allow teachers to identify rather quickly where learners are failing to include crucial information or are including too much detail. It provides a key to those points in written accounts where native speakers use pronouns (for example, *she*, *it*) more than nouns (for example, *the woman*, *the bottle*) for subsequent reference. In short, it provides a basic analytic key, derived from a study of performance variation, for the description of what both native speakers and learners of a language actually do in the production of one type of written discourse.

Native speakers aren't perfect
While we have been able to illustrate, in Table 2.5, the variety of forms used in these simple narratives, those forms still represent a level of

abstraction away from the type of variation that can be found via more detailed analysis of the formation of complex expressions. In the final scene of the narrative, the child places the bottle in a particular location. The descriptions of that location by our subjects can serve to illustrate a type of variation in native speaker use of English which, as far as we know, is never presented in ESL teaching materials. This type of variation involves the use of 'errors'—formally incorrect expressions. Since one of the assumptions at issue is the idea that native speakers have perfect command of their language, we wanted to make sure that the 'errors' we uncovered in our initial fifty-subject sample were not a trivial feature of careless performance by a few individuals on the task. Using the same materials and procedure, we increased our population (more subjects with exactly the same profile as presented earlier) to a total of 214 subjects. The analysis of this extended sample concentrated only on expressions used to describe the final location of the bottle in the narratives. Two basic constructions were used and these are shown, with the variant forms used in the major construction, in Table 2.6.

Construction	Number	Percentage
'the'	5	2.3
'her'	4	1.9
'Mrs Smith's'	18	8.4
'the lady's'	22	10.3
'the woman's'	57	26.6
'her mother's friend's'	4	1.9
Subtotal	110	51.4
'Mrs Smith'	5	2.3
'the lady'	2	0.9
'the ladys'	4	1.9
'the ladies'	27	12.6
'the woman'	3	1.4
'the womans'	32	15.0
'the womens'	8	3.7
'the women's'	3	1.4
'her mother's friends'	3	1.4
Subtotal	87	40.6
'in the bag/purse of the woman/lady'	17	8.0
Total	214	

Table 2.6 Constructions used in referring to Location 3:
'in (Character 1's) bag/purse'

In Table 2.6, it is clear that the most common expression used to mark possession (*the woman's*) is formed correctly and that, overall, correct forms outnumber incorrect forms. However, the second and third most frequent expressions (i.e. *the womans*; *the ladies*) are formed incorrectly. And, in fact, forty per cent of the forms produced by these native speakers were incorrect.

Some might argue that native speaker variation can be expected in larger 'communicative' pieces of discourse like narratives, but would not occur in ESL tasks limited to a focus upon grammatical form. We would suggest that this is not the case—that native speaker variation can be expected in all sorts of language tasks. For example, in Tarone (1985), several native speakers failed to achieve 100 per cent accuracy in their scores on a paper-and-pencil test which asked them to judge the grammaticality of sentences lacking obligatory articles, plural markers, and third person singular verb markers; this was variability which resulted in error. We argue throughout this book that the teacher should, as a matter of course, try out all foreign language tasks on native speakers in order to establish a baseline against which to measure learner performance. How do native speakers (who are not language teachers) complete a particular cloze passage, or answer questions on a reading? How do they fill in the blanks in a grammar exercise?

The finding that native speakers of English often produce incorrect forms may prove disturbing to many English teachers, among others, but that is not the point we are trying to make. We simply wish to illustrate the existence of variation, even in written language performance, among a native speaker population whose linguistic production skills would not represent an unreasonable target for the vast majority of ESL learners. We are not suggesting that incorrect written forms be presented as models for learners. However, we would like to emphasize that, if variation of this type does exist, learners should not be encouraged to believe that the native speaker competence which they may be seeking to achieve is some ideal, perfect, and uniform phenomenon. What learners need is an awareness of the range and type of variation that exists in native speaker performance. In practical terms, we believe that this awareness should come from a range of experiences with elicited native speaker data. A means of acquiring those data, as part of the language learning process, is consequently built into Exercises 2 and 3, presented for use by classroom teachers, in Appendix 2.

6 Review of techniques

To summarize, then, in this part of the book we have described four levels of needs analysis and suggested a number of techniques which a classroom teacher might use to gather data on language use in the 'outside world'. For the convenience of the reader we summarize below that set of data-gathering techniques, organized roughly in terms of the amount of teacher time and energy required, from least effort (1) to most effort (10).

1 Develop and distribute a language use questionnaire to each class on the first day of class. Determine learner aims and language-related activities in situations requiring the target language.
2 Give class assignments in Appendix 2.
3 Assign students to gather data on their own language needs in particular situations, by means of interviews, questionnaires, collection of realia, as in Appendix 1, or tape-recordings of interactions.
4 Collect and organize several sets of data gathered in (3) above. Use in lessons.
5 Write to or telephone fluent speakers who habitually interact with learners in target situations; interview them, administer questionnaires, request copies of documents, forms, corrected papers, etc.
6 Interview fluent speakers a second time, asking about the information obtained in (5).
7 Go to the site of the target situation to interview fluent speakers as in (5) and (6) above.
8 Tape-record role-played interactions between fluent speakers, or between learners and fluent speakers in the target situation. Use recordings in class.
9 Tape-record actual interactions as in (8) above.
10 Transcribe and analyze recordings obtained in (8) and (9) above.

These techniques will be productive for language teachers interested in gaining more direct information about the language needs of their students. The data obtained by means of most of the techniques will be doubly useful to the teacher: first, in planning a syllabus and selecting points to be taught, and second, in providing authentic data for use in classroom exercises.

In this part, we have presented an approach to the analysis of what learners need to know, based upon the communicative behavior of fluent speakers of the language in situations like those in which the learners participate. However, a thorough needs analysis should not stop here. In order to teach effectively, the classroom teacher also needs to determine what it is that the learners do and do not already know about the language. We turn to this issue in Part Three.

Further reading

For a very helpful model of the factors which may be considered in a detailed analysis of the communicative needs of any learner, see Munby (1978). Yalden (1987) presents a set of frameworks for teacher-conducted needs surveys. A more global account of the processes involved in course design at the system level, including those of needs analysis, can be found in Dubin and Olshtain (1986). General texts on language needs analysis are Buckingham (1981) and Richterich (1983). An excellent discussion of the role of learners' aims is presented in Widdowson (1983). A critique of specialist-executed needs analysis may be found in Hutchinson and Waters (1980).

Research on LSP and ESP is reported in the *ESP Journal*, the *ESP Newsletter*, and *ESPMENA Bulletin*, as well as in a variety of other language journals. A collection of papers on ESP appears in Selinker *et al.* (1981), and a valuable annotated collection of papers on ESP, presented in a historical perspective with very helpful commentary provided by the editor, appears in Swales (1985). A recent handbook on the subject is Hutchinson and Waters (1987). For perspectives on the rhetorical community concept, particularly in English for Academic Purposes, see the contributions in Connor and Kaplan (1987), Horowitz (1986), Johns (1988), or Purves and Purves (1986). For examples of global-level needs analysis, see Mackay (1981) and Sorensen (1982), and for examples of a grammatical–rhetorical analysis, refer to Lackstrom, Selinker, and Trimble (1972), Oster (1981), Tarone *et al.* (1981), and Williams (1988). Myers (1989) argues convincingly that many of the grammatical features of scientific writing can be explained in terms of politeness conventions used in making and denying claims. Examples of analysis at the grammatical level are Swales (1976), Cooray (1967), and George (1963). Scotton and Bernsten (1988) argue for the use of naturally-occurring native speaker data in classroom materials, and describe a study which provides a model to follow in obtaining these data.

PART THREE

What learners do and do not know

Introduction

In deciding what to teach a particular class, it is not enough to establish those aspects of the target language which the learners need to know. An investigation must also be carried out to determine the degree to which the learners in that class already know the target language. The study of learner language has mushroomed in recent years, and second language acquisition is now an important field of study in applied linguistics. Yet, while much has been learned about the ways in which a second language learner's communicative abilities develop, our knowledge in this area is still incomplete. There is much that classroom teachers must discover for themselves about any particular group of students' abilities.

Typically, an analysis of what a group of learners knows about the language takes place before the learners ever enter the classroom: students are given standardized proficiency tests designed by specialists.

Such proficiency tests, however, do not always meet the needs of the classroom teacher or the students. The fact is that most standardized proficiency tests measure only a limited aspect of the student's knowledge of the second language, and often do not measure those aspects which are taught in, for example, communicative syllabuses. Thus, it is not uncommon for language programs these days to follow a communicative syllabus, in which goals and objectives are functional skills—yet for learners in these same programs to be 'placed' in classes on the basis of their score on a measure of grammatical ability. While designers of standardized proficiency tests are of course aware of the problem and are working to develop measures of communicative skills, these are not yet included in most programs. Teachers in the classroom typically analyze their students' communicative abilities in the language intuitively.

It is generally agreed by theorists in this area that a thorough analysis of what learners know should involve not just linguistic competence in the language, but communicative competence. In Chapter 2 and in the Introduction to Part Two (see in particular Table 2.1), we have cited Canale and Swain's (1980) analysis of communicative competence as involving at least the three components of grammatical, sociolinguistic, and strategic competence. For convenience, we will summarize this analysis again here.

Grammatical competence involves knowledge about the phonological and grammatical structure, or *form*, of the language, and the ability to produce and understand those forms in speech and writing. So, for example, an achievement test which assesses a learner's ability to use rules for constructing 'yes/no' questions in the second language is designed to be a measure of that learner's grammatical competence. It is this aspect of communicative competence which is most successfully measured by standardized proficiency tests.

Sociolinguistic competence involves the ability to produce and understand language which is appropriate to specific social situations and conforms to the politeness conventions of those situations. A test which required students to enact a role play in which they apologized to a friend in an appropriate manner would be a measure of sociolinguistic competence.

Strategic competence is the ability to successfully transmit information in the language—as, for example, the ability to describe a referent so that a hearer can correctly identify it. Strategic competence is directly tied to the ability to use communication strategies to cope with difficulties which arise in the course of getting one's message across to particular listeners—for example, when one does not know a needed vocabulary item. A test which asks learners to give directions clearly so that a hearer can successfully make his or her way from the railway station to the hotel is a measure of strategic competence.

While all three components of communicative competence are clearly related (for example, unless one has some minimal grammatical competence in the second language, one will be unlikely to have very extensive mastery of appropriate and polite social formulae in that language), it is clear that they *can* develop rather independently as a learner acquires a second language. For example, learners can know a great deal about the grammatical structure of French as a second language, yet be unable to use the language to get themselves from the bus depot to the hotel in France (primarily a matter of strategic competence), or to apologize in a manner which native French speakers would find acceptable and polite (primarily a function of sociolinguistic competence). Or, to take another example, a learner may be quite effective at transmitting information in the second language, but always with a great many grammatical errors; in this case, strategic competence is better developed than grammatical competence in the language.

In the chapters which follow, we discuss the means which classroom teachers can use to determine their students' abilities in terms of each of the three components of communicative competence. We will examine first the area of grammatical competence, then sociolinguistic competence, and finally strategic competence. We provide sample instruments, where feasible, to be used in the investigation of students' abilities in each of these three areas.

7 Grammatical competence

1 Investigating grammatical competence

Determining what learners do and do not know in the area of grammatical competence would seem, on first consideration, to be a relatively straightforward matter. There is, after all, a very long tradition of linguistic analysis which has been devoted to the identification of the grammatical components of a language. If learners can demonstrate that they 'know' the rules, then they must surely possess grammatical competence. Unfortunately, this apparently straightforward relationship hardly survives as a practical notion once a number of theoretical and methodological issues have been raised. In this section we shall explore the advantages and disadvantages of several different methods which have been used to investigate grammatical competence. In the next section, we shall consider some recent evidence which suggests that no single method will provide a characterization of what, for second language learners, must be a variable system which will tend to provide evidence of different levels of knowledge under different performance conditions. The key issue throughout this discussion is what counts as ways of 'demonstrating knowledge'. Let us consider some of the ways.

Stating the rules

For the ancients, grammatical knowledge seems to have been demonstrated by the ability to state a series of rules. For centuries, the form in which knowledge of the rules of Latin as a second language could be demonstrated essentially followed a pattern laid down around AD 350 in the *Ars Minor* of the Roman grammarian, Donatus. Here is an extract from the translated version by Salus:

Q: How many degrees of comparison are there?
A: Three.
Q: What?
A: Positive, as learned; comparative, as more learned; superlative, as most learned.
Q: What nouns are compared?
A: Only common nouns signifying quality or quantity.
Q: What case is the comparative degree used with?
A: The ablative without a preposition; for we say "doctior illo".

Q: What case with the superlative?
A: Only the genitive plural; for we say "doctissimus poetarum".
(Salus 1969:92)

Even today, there seem to be some learners who approach the task of second language learning as one in which the ability to state grammatical rules is the perceived goal. Unfortunately, this kind of explicit knowledge about the language does not necessarily guarantee ability to use the language with grammatical accuracy. Most ESL teachers will be familiar with learners whose previous instruction in English has provided them with extensive knowledge, encoded in technical vocabulary, as to how the English language is to be described. There is an inevitable first impression that such learners must possess an advanced level of grammatical competence. Quite often, this impression does not survive beyond an encounter with the learners' extended written or spoken production in class. However, even if we did find that grammatical accuracy in production occasionally accompanied learners' ability to state grammatical rules, we would still be rather cautious about using this 'explicit statement' method as a reliable guide. We know that very few native speakers can state the grammatical rules of their language. We should also keep in mind the fact that, in recent years, particularly in ESL teaching contexts in the United States and Britain, there has been much less emphasis on explicit 'rule learning' as a classroom practice. Consequently, we should expect that relatively few learners from these contexts, even those who have developed native-like skills in actually using the second language, will have any familiarity with the explicit form of more than a few grammatical rules. Indeed, when learners' personal accounts of what they know are reported, we tend to find statements like the following, from Cohen and Robbins (1976:59): 'I guess I just never learned the rules that well. I know that every time I speak it's pretty correct, so I never think about grammars. I just write down whatever I feel like it.' This particular learner's background had not included much formal grammatical instruction. Some learners, on the other hand, may have had, particularly in a foreign language learning situation, a great deal of exposure to the traditional grammar book. Yet, we should remain aware of the fact that many traditional grammar-book rules are prescriptive, rather than descriptive, of what contemporary language users actually do. We have observed classroom situations in which an ESL learner has tried to explain to the teacher why an English sentence the teacher used must be ungrammatical (according to some rule), while the teacher responds with, 'Well, that's just how we say it'. The learner never seems to be convinced. It may be that the explicit knowledge of traditional grammatical rules of a language actually interferes with the acquisition or development of ability to use the language with native-like competence. Consequently, we might be rather cautious about treating a learner's explicit statement of grammatical rules as a reliable guide in investigating his or her grammatical competence.

Discrete-point and integrative measures

Most methods of investigating a learner's grammatical competence try to determine the extent of that learner's implicit knowledge. The best-known formats involve what is known as discrete-point testing. In these formats, learners are required to demonstrate their knowledge on one point of grammar at a time, and the sum of performance on those individual points (assuming we have identified all those that are relevant) will represent overall ability. Since anyone who has been involved in learning or teaching a second or foreign language in any way during the past twenty years will have met multiple-choice or fill-in-the-blank exercises or tests, we shall not describe these formats here. (The strongest promotion of these measures can be found in Lado 1961, and guidance on how to construct different types of items is offered in Heaton 1975.)

The large-scale use of these formats is testimony to their perceived value as a means of investigating grammatical knowledge. Discrete-point test items can be constructed quite easily, administered with little effort, and scored very rapidly. They can be used to isolate specific aspects of syntax, morphology, phonology, or lexis to determine what elements of the language the learners have trouble with. They are, quite simply, excellent formats for assessing isolated aspects of the second language. They may, however, be rather misleading measures of overall grammatical competence.

To understand this distinction which is drawn between a learner's ability on discrete-point items and his or her overall ability, we have to consider arguments presented on behalf of what is called integrative testing. Instead of investigating knowledge as a series of single discrete elements, an integrative measure tries to investigate the learner's ability to use many aspects of the language at the same time. Whereas discrete-point items appear in minimal linguistic contexts, integrative measures employ extended discourse contexts. The distinction between the measures is often expressed as the difference between the structuralist view of language (a piece of language represents the sum of its individual parts), and a pragmatic view (a piece of language as a whole relates to an interpretation which has extra-linguistic connections and is inevitably more than the sum of its parts). Consequently, the argument goes, we use our grammatical competence, in real life, to produce and to comprehend meaningful discourse, not to decide which item (from sets of alternative forms) will be correct in one single decontextualized test sentence after another. It may also happen that some students, on the basis of their particular training, become highly skilled at choosing correct answers on discrete-point test items, yet otherwise display very little skill in producing or understanding the language.

The most common formats for integrative measurement are dictation and cloze procedures, employing extended chunks of discourse in the second language. In a cloze procedure, for example, such a chunk of discourse, with every *n*th word (for example, every sixth or seventh word) deleted and replaced by a blank, is presented to the learner. The learner's ability to accurately replace the deleted words or to supply appropriate alternatives is taken to be a measure of his or her grammatical competence. In a dictation procedure, learners hear extended oral discourse (presented of course in short chunks), and write down what they hear. Dictation and cloze measures thus allow one to determine a learner's ability to both comprehend and produce the language in the context of meaningful discourse. An additional advantage of these integrative test formats is that, if the teacher wishes to investigate specific aspects of the learners' ability to produce grammatically accurate forms, then the fill-in-the-blank and multiple-choice designs can be incorporated into modified versions of the dictation and cloze procedures in investigating learners' mastery of syntax, morphology, or lexis. (Oller 1979 provides discussion and illustration of a range of options.) Thus, a text which includes a number of verbs in the past tense can be modified, either with blanks or a set of alternative forms, at each point where a past tense verb occurs. The ability of the learner to restore the text to its original form or another appropriate form may provide a measure of his or her knowledge of the past tense. If the texts employed are chosen from a content area or subject matter (for example, physics, agronomy, medicine, etc.) which is representative of the learner's target repertoire, then quite specialized learner needs can be determined by means of such formats. Of course, when tests like the cloze are used as diagnostic tests, they may be very hard to interpret, simply because they are so complex. It is here in particular that native speaker data may be helpful. Asking native speakers (or, in an EFL setting, fluent speakers) to perform the same cloze or dictation tests, and using their performance as a baseline, may be very helpful to teachers who are attempting to accurately diagnose their students' needs by using these measures. In short, the use of integrative exercises and tests offers great potential benefits for discovering what aspects of the grammar of the target language learners know.

The major drawback of any such measure, from multiple-choice to cloze test, is its link to a particular view of the language learning process. Invariably, the learner's language is described in terms of what aspects of the target language the learner has or has not mastered. Yet, it has become apparent that such a description provides a relatively poor picture of the fairly complex process involved in the evolution of a learner's grammatical competence. Corder has stated the issue in the following way:

> The principal defect of tests is that they ask the wrong question from our point of view: does the learner know this or that category of the target language? Can he perform this or that process in the target language? ... Tests are not devised to ask the question: what does the learner know? What are the rules he is using and the systems and categories he is working with?
> (Corder 1981:60)

We believe that Corder's alternative questions are much more pertinent to the study of the learner's competence, and, throughout the rest of this chapter, we shall concentrate on describing ways to investigate what learners know from this alternative perspective.

The impetus for asking these alternative questions was the recognition that each learner operates with a linguistic system, called an 'interlanguage' (Selinker 1972), which is distinct from the systems of both the first and second languages. To describe any learner's grammatical competence is consequently a matter of describing a particular state of his or her interlanguage as a system in its own right, rather than making a list of statements concerning identified aspects of the target language. A common means employed in investigating this rather different concept of grammatical competence is found in the grammaticality judgment exercise.

Grammaticality judgments and making corrections

The strongest claim made on behalf of the grammaticality judgment type of exercise is that 'judgments of grammaticality provide better data for the study of a person's knowledge of his language than do actual utterances of the speaker' (Baker 1978:12). While preferring to use the term 'acceptability judgment', Newmeyer also claims that an English speaker's ability to make such judgments to distinguish between syntactically well-formed and ill-formed sentences 'no doubt reflects fairly directly their linguistic competence' (1983:51). If it is the case that native speaker judgments provide some fairly direct reflection of (linguistic) competence, and are more revealing than the native speaker's utterances, then it is hardly surprising that some second language researchers (for example, Adjémian 1981) have assumed that the same relationship exists for second language learners.

The motivation for using language users' intuitions stems from claims in the early work of Chomsky (1957, 1964) that the adequacy of a generative grammar could be determined via speakers' judgments of the grammaticality of the products of that grammar. Although such claims have been seriously disputed, in both theoretical and empirical terms (for example, Labov 1975; Maclay and Sleator 1960), the technique of eliciting intuitional judgments has continued to be used for various practical purposes in second language research. Whether or not one believes that such exercises provide a 'direct reflection of competence' (and we shall provide some evidence indicating the contrary in Part Four of this book), it is clear that grammaticality judgment exercises are an extremely useful method for providing teachers with some insight into what their learners *perceive* to be grammatical. From a needs analysis point of view, such perceptions are extremely important. As Arthur has pointed out, it may be the case that 'the "errors" made by second language learners are, from the learner's own perspective, not errors at all' (1980:178); in other words, they are consistent with systematic rules of the learner's own interlanguage. It is just that the learner's rules are not the same as the target language rules. Consequently, if an ESL learner identifies well-formed English sentences as ungrammatical and ill-formed sentences as grammatical, then the teacher may have discovered an aspect of the learner's interlanguage which will seriously interfere with any further development toward ability to use the second language effectively.

While many studies employing learners' intuitions have sought to investigate a range of general or theoretical issues (cf. Chaudron 1983 for a review), the classroom teacher will typically have a much more narrowly-focussed goal. For example, after several sessions on the structure and use of English relative clauses, an ESL teacher noted that, in their written work, a large number of learners continued to produce a range of ungrammatical relative clause structures. These examples from the learners' own production provided an obvious data set for the teacher to use in a grammaticality judgment exercise. Also included in the exercise was a set of well-formed structures corresponding to the identified ungrammatical structures. Thus, the learners were asked to judge the grammaticality of sets of sentences like the following:

OK/NOT OK 1 The boy who was waiting outside had a broken arm.
OK/NOT OK 2 The man was sitting next to me talked a lot about the weather.
OK/NOT OK 3 The student listening to his radio didn't hear the bell.
OK/NOT OK 4 The girl who watching television laughed a lot.

The identified errors which had been found in these students' work involved omission of the relative pronoun, as in (2), and omission of the auxiliary, as in (4). The corresponding correct target language forms were included as (1) and (3). The interesting result of this informal classroom exercise was that the vast majority decided that (1), (2), and (4) were correct, and that (3) was incorrect. The ESL teacher, finding this result, immediately suspected that it was caused by an emphasis, in the teaching materials, on converting separate full sentences to embedded relative clauses by using the relative pronoun. That is, the students had performed this familiar type of exercise many times:

The student fell and hurt himself.
The student was running.
The student who was running fell and hurt himself.

The teacher surmised that these students judged (3) to be ungrammatical because it lacked a relative pronoun and auxiliary: *who was*. The question which remained was: if the students had been shown, in class, the basic elements of this type of structure, why were they not recognizing the errors in (2) and (4), which also resulted from omission of parts of the structure?

A second exercise used the same format, but, following a procedure that has become quite common in reported research, learners were asked first to identify each incorrect structure and then to 'make it correct' by writing in the necessary changes. The aim of this exercise was to gain some insight into what elements in this type of structure were perceived by these learners to be necessary for grammaticality. (A fuller version of this type of exercise, with instructions, is presented in Appendix 3, for use as a guide in constructing other, comparable exercises.)

OK/NOT OK 5 The teachers who were coming by bus arrived late.
OK/NOT OK 6 The people were leaving that night packed their bags early.
OK/NOT OK 7 The doctors working in that hospital didn't have much free time.
OK/NOT OK 8 The professors who teaching those courses gave a lot of assignments.

In performing this exercise, some learners produced individual corrections such as adding *and* between *night* and *packed* in (6) and adding *they* between *courses* and *gave* in (8). However, more generally, all students identified (7) as incorrect and the majority (60 per cent) corrected it by adding *who were* between *doctors* and *working*. One group (20 per cent) only added *were* and a different group (20 per cent) added only *who*. The general pattern which emerges here is that these students seem to treat the full relative clause structure (relative pronoun *plus* auxiliary) as the most desirable, yet will accept any one of the two elements (relative pronoun *or* auxiliary) as sufficient for structural correctness. This speculation serves to identify a possible aspect of these students' interlanguage grammar which will potentially lead them to produce both correct and incorrect relative clause structures, perceiving them to be correct, and not to produce correct 'reduced' relative clause structures (as exemplified by (3) and (7)), because they perceive them to be incorrect.

Identifying this pattern in the students' perception of grammaticality can be treated as a first step in describing a possible 'rule' of their interlanguage which might account for systematic variability in their written English production. Stated as a hypothesis, this informal finding could then form the basis of a controlled piece of research (carried out, perhaps, by a graduate student or researcher) which might use a large number of examples and a substantial population of learners (with identified backgrounds and proficiency levels) to yield a justifiable claim about the nature of the interlanguage systems of some ESL learners.

However, of more immediate relevance for the classroom teacher is the elicited information that these learners have obvious misperceptions concerning English relative clause forms. The set of sentences used in the exercise, together with the students' 'corrections', might then serve as a basis for a class discussion on the learners' reasons for their choices. If the teacher can also present the same four sentences with the 'corrections' provided by a group of native speakers, then the discussion might lead to an identification of the mismatch between the learners' 'rules' for English relative clauses and the 'rules' which native speakers must be using.

The key to this type of exercise is the recognition, by the classroom teacher, of a specific problem—whether phonological, grammatical, morphological, or lexical—experienced by a particular group of learners. Throughout this section, we have considered typical investigative measures which do not require the learner to produce much language. By themselves, without additional information about learners' production of the language, such measures—far from reflecting 'fairly directly their linguistic competence'—may provide a limited, potentially misleading, picture of what learners know. In the following section, we shall try to illustrate this point in more detail.

2 Variability in learner language

As we have just noted, it is important to investigate not only the ability of language students to make grammaticality judgments in their second language, but also their ability to *produce* that language, in either oral or written form. While there are many commercially produced tests of learner proficiency and achievement which can give the instructor an idea of the approximate level of the students in a classroom, these are usually not precise enough for the purposes of the language teacher. The teacher, in designing a lesson plan, wishes to know what it is that his or her students know about some grammatical feature of the target language. For this purpose, in-class evaluation seems appropriate.

For example, let us suppose that a teacher of English as a second language is beginning a unit on English articles with a group of students, and wishes to determine whether they can produce articles accurately.

Typically, he or she may prepare a diagnostic test, possibly a multiple-choice test which forces students to indicate whether an article is needed in front of a noun phrase, and if so, which article, *the* or *alan*. On the basis of the students' performance on this task, the teacher will decide whether the students are able to produce articles accurately. That decision on the basis of the diagnostic test results may determine how much class time is devoted to presentation and practice on article usage.

The use of such classroom diagnostic tests to evaluate grammatical competence is relatively uncontroversial, although teachers may disagree on the *type* of test to use. As we have seen, some practitioners argue that, instead of a multiple-choice test on articles, a cloze test might be more appropriate, since it presents the student with a more natural discourse context. But diagnostic classroom tests are here to stay. While most teachers realize that such traditional tests are not an accurate reflection of a student's ability to use the language in real life, nevertheless most of them believe that there is a *predictable relationship* between students' scores on a written grammar test, and their grammatical accuracy when speaking or writing in the second language. There is a general belief that a student's grammatical accuracy on a classroom test, either discrete-point or integrative, will be *higher* than his or her accuracy in more 'communicative' tasks, so that if the student achieves, say, seventy-five per cent accuracy on the grammar test measuring article usage, he or she will probably achieve a lower accuracy rate on more 'communicative' tasks like classroom debates, oral narratives, and so on.

One or two students may challenge this assumption, claiming that, although they have not achieved a perfect score on the teacher's diagnostic test, they do produce articles accurately in communicative situations. Without any means to verify these claims, language teachers tend to have to dismiss them and get on with teaching their planned unit on articles.

However, recent research on task-related variation in grammatical accuracy suggests that the students, and not the teacher, may have the more accurate view in this case. The results of this research have important implications for interpreting test results in the area of grammatical form, and should be taken into consideration by classroom teachers interested in obtaining a better understanding of their students' abilities to produce grammatical forms accurately in a second language. We will now take a look at some of this research.

Degrees of accuracy

Evidence now accumulating in the research literature shows that second language learners produce grammatical forms with differing degrees of accuracy, depending on the nature of the task they are performing. That is, the accuracy of learner language is *variable,* and this variability has been shown to be related to the sort of task used to elicit learner productions.

Research evidence on variation in interlanguage is described and evaluated in Tarone (1988). For example, researchers like the Dickersons (1974, 1975, 1976, 1977) and Beebe (1980) have amassed data on variable phonology in the second language. A typical finding is that from Dickerson and Dickerson (1977) in Figure 3.1 which shows that Japanese learners of English produced /r/ with varying degrees of correctness, depending on whether they were speaking freely, reading a dialogue, or reading a word list—tasks which are assumed to demand increasing attention to form. Correct production of /r/ in the target language occurred most frequently in careful speech and least frequently in casual speech.

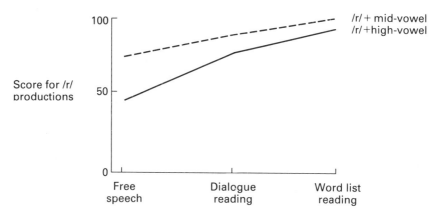

Figure 3.1   Correct production of /r/ in two contexts: (1) /r/ + mid-vowel and (2) /r/ + high-vowel (Dickerson and Dickerson 1977)

Data are also available on inherent variability in the grammar and morphology of a second language. For example, Schmidt (1980) found that advanced learners from several native language backgrounds varied in their treatment of a rule allowing second-verb ellipsis in English, in sentences like

Mary is eating an apple and Sue ø a pear.

In investigating the status of this rule in the second language, English, Schmidt asked her subjects to perform four tasks.

In Table 3.1, we see that these learners *never* produced second-verb ellipsis in an oral production task (learners were asked to describe fifteen pictures of situations with redundant elements). When asked to repeat sentences like the example given above a few seconds after a native speaker of English in an elicited imitation task, eleven per cent could

	Free oral production	Elicited imitation	Written sentence-combining	Grammatical judgment
Second-verb deletion rates	0%	11%	25%	50%

Table 3.1   Variable second-verb deletion in four elicitation tasks for nine learners of ESL (from data in Schmidt 1980)

repeat it exactly (most of the others supplied the missing verb). When asked to combine (in writing) two sentences with identical verbs (for example: 'Marvin plays the violin. Louise plays the piano'), twenty-five per cent deleted the second verb. And, when asked to say whether sentences like the example were grammatical in English, fifty per cent said they were. So these four different elicitation tasks seem to provide us with four different pictures of the status of this rule in the learners' second language; this variability is systematic, with the frequency of occurrence of sentences like the example given increasing gradually from more casual free speech to more careful grammatical judgments.

A more complex pattern of variation was found in a full-scale study of variation in learners' grammatical accuracy at the level of syntax and morphology (Tarone 1985). We describe this study here in some detail, not because we expect that teachers will want to replicate it, but because the results should be of considerable relevance to teachers interested in evaluating their students' grammatical competence.

Twenty second-language learners participated in this study, all of them adults learning English as a Second Language at the advanced level. Ten subjects were native speakers of Arabic and ten were native speakers of Japanese.

Chosen for study was the presence or absence in obligatory contexts of four target language forms: third person singular present tense verb -s; the articles *a/an* and *the*; the noun plural -s, and third person singular direct object pronouns.

Three tasks were performed by the learners:

Task 1: a written grammaticality judgment task consisting of thirty English sentences. Learners were asked to star any sentence which was grammatically incorrect, and to rewrite the erroneous portion correctly. This task was assumed to require the most careful performance of the learners and was expected to elicit the grammar forms with highest accuracy.

Task 2: an oral interview with a native speaker of English, focussing on the topic of the learners' field of study at the university, plans for academic work in the United States, and plans to apply that work in their own country. It was assumed that grammatical accuracy on this task would fall somewhere between that on the grammar test and in the narrative.

Task 3: an oral narrative task (see Appendix B) which required learners to look at a sequence of events depicted on a video screen nonverbally, and then to 'tell the story' to a non-native listener who had not seen the video. (Japanese and Arabic speakers were paired for this task.) The listener had to select the correct picture sequence from three sets of still photographs representing the story. On the basis of previous experience with narrative tasks like this, it was assumed that the learners would pay the least attention to grammatical form and that their grammatical accuracy would 'be lowest on this task.

The learners' oral communications in the interview and narrative were tape-recorded and transcribed.

The learners' accuracy in using the four grammatical forms on the written grammar test, and on the oral interview and narrative, was then determined (see Tarone 1985 for details of the method used to calculate accuracy). The results are displayed overleaf in Figure 3.2.

It was found that the learners' *judgment* of three target language forms on the written grammar test varied markedly from their accuracy in *using* those same forms in the oral communication tasks. Only the plural morpheme (and, for the Japanese, the third person marker) seem to have been produced at approximately the same rate of accuracy on the grammar test as on the two oral tasks.

The variability in the learners' production of the third person singular present tense -s occurred in a pattern which we might, as teachers, expect; the learners were most accurate on the grammar test and least accurate on the oral narrative. However, the article and the direct object pronoun *it* show exactly the opposite pattern; for both these forms, there was *less* grammatical accuracy on the grammar test than on either of the oral communication tasks. In addition, of the two oral tasks, the one which had been thought to demand the least attention to language form, the narrative, showed the highest accuracy rates for these two grammatical forms.

One of the Japanese learners, for example, missed two of the three questions on the written grammar test which related to direct object pronouns: he incorrectly accepted these two sentences as grammatical:

1 She took the picture and put on the bulletin board.
2 I won't know what is in the package until I receive.

He accurately corrected the third sentence:

3 He took the ball and threw *it* to Tom.

On the oral narrative task, however, this same learner *never* omitted a direct object pronoun:

4 … just to take a glance at the textbook, and she was reading *it* …
5 … she put the textbook on, on her bag. She left *it*.
6 … and she also took *it* out …
7 … she put *it* into the bag …

This learner, then, achieved an accuracy rate of 33 per cent on the written grammar test and of 100 per cent in the oral narrative task in his use of direct object pronouns in an obligatory context. Similar patterns were found across the entire group of twenty learners. Thus, these findings provide some evidence that second language users treated different sets of grammatical forms differently under identical task conditions. Some forms (like noun plural -s) did not seem to shift at all across judgment and production tasks. Some (like third person singular present tense -s) seemed to occur with greatest accuracy on the grammar test. And the accuracy rates of some (for example, articles and direct object pronouns) were actually lowest on that same grammar test.

The results of the study are important, both theoretically and practically. First, these findings must lead us to question any assumption that we will get a 'direct reflection of competence' by asking learners to judge the grammaticality of target language sentences. As we pointed out in the last section, such judgments tell us only what learners perceive to be grammatical, and, unless supplemented by information about their ability to produce the language, may provide a limited, potentially misleading picture of what they know. The findings of the study just reported raise important questions about the possibility of directly measuring a learner's grammatical *competence* by means of perceptual tasks alone; perhaps researchers need to focus more on obtaining accurate descriptions of learners' productive *performance* on various measures before inferring much about the structure of 'underlying competence'.

On a more practical (but related) level, we must conclude that if variability in learner language follows this pattern, some questions are raised for achievement and proficiency testing. In this study, performance on a written grammar test did not seem to be a very good predictor of the learners' ability to use the tested grammatical forms correctly in at least two types of oral discourse. Teachers and testers have always assumed that written grammar tests have some predictable relationship to the grammar rules a learner uses in actually communicating in the target language. But the results of this study raise serious questions about the validity of this assumption—the assumption seems to hold true for some grammatical forms but not for others.

Why is it that these learners produced articles and the direct object pronoun *least* accurately on the written test while at the same time they produced third person singular markers *most* accurately on that same test?

The influence of cohesion and communicative pressure

We should point out that, at the same time that these tasks have been ordered in terms of (expected) decreasing amount of attention to

Figure 3.2   Grammatical accuracy on four English forms by two groups of ESL learners on three tasks: written grammar test, oral interview, and oral narrative (Tarone 1985)

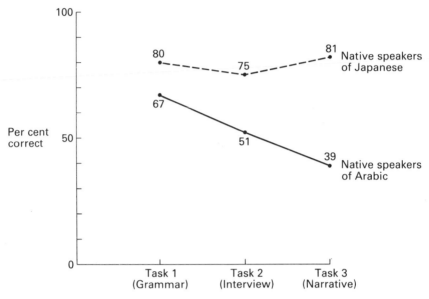

Third person singular present tense verb-s

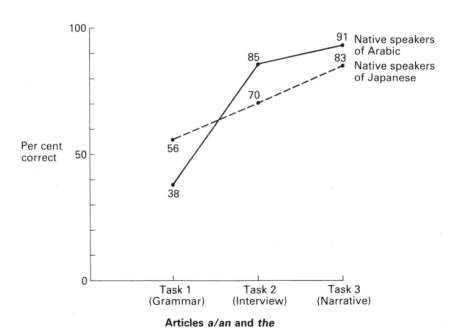

Articles *a/an* and *the*

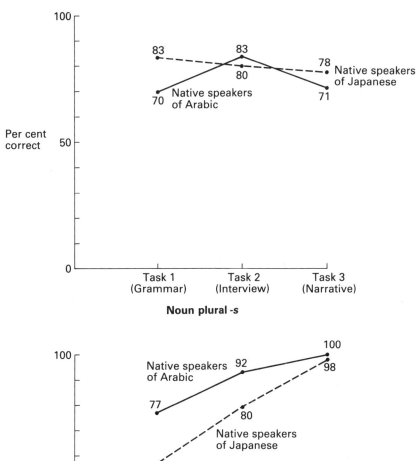

Noun plural -s

Direct object pronoun *it*

grammatical form (grammar test, oral interview, oral narrative), they have also been ordered according to at least two other criteria as well: (1) the connectedness of the discourse involved in the task, and (2) the communicative pressure placed upon the speaker to transmit information clearly. That is, the grammar test, which had been thought to require most attention to language form, consists of unconnected sentences. There is no cohesiveness at all beyond the sentence level. Furthermore, there is no premium placed in this task upon the clarity of the information presented. The narrative task (see Appendix 7), which had been thought to involve least attention to language form, requires the speaker to produce a form of discourse which has many cohesive ties and which puts the speaker in total control of the discourse for an extended and predictable period of time. Furthermore, on the narrative task there was a listener who had a clear need to know the information being presented in the narrative; the *listener* had a task to complete which depended upon the *speaker's* ability to transmit information clearly. In the interview, while speakers could produce extended bits of discourse, their turns could also be interrupted at unpredictable intervals by the interviewer with a resulting disruption of the speaker's control over extended cohesive ties. Further, the interviewer did not have a clear need to know the information being presented by the speaker; there was every possibility that the interviewer was simply listening out of politeness. In short, there was an inverse relationship in the study between the degree of attention to language form thought to be required by these tasks, and, among other characteristics, the cohesiveness of the discourse elicited by them and the degree of communicative pressure placed upon the speaker.

How can these observations account for the fact that the accuracy rates of different language forms shifted in different directions on the same sequence of tasks? It can be argued that both the article and the direct object pronoun *it* (which became more accurate as tasks required more cohesive discourse) are forms which are more important in establishing cohesiveness in discourse and in keeping track of referents than, for example, the third person singular marker (which became less accurate as tasks required more cohesive discourse). In fact, in spoken discourse, the third person singular marker is largely redundant. In successfully narrating a story, however, the speaker must make sure that references to the various protagonists and objects which are crucial to the story line are clear; articles and pronouns are very important in maintaining this sort of clear reference. The following transcript of the narrative produced by one of the learners in this study may be helpful in illustrating the way in which the learners worked to maintain clear reference on the narrative task.

1 This story was in the in the class—the—teacher

2 came, it was a woman, the teacher came, and he came
3 first and he put—his book—in the desk, and when
4 he went to write—on the blackboard, one student
5 came—and—he didn't find anything to do, and he
6 took—one magazine or one magazine from the teacher's
7 desk, and write it—uh and uh want to—to saw some
8 pictures, and he put it in his—in his desk, the
9 student put the magazine in his desk, and he—and he
10 go back, and one other student came. He sit, he sat
11 behind—the place—of the first, and he take the
12 magazine, and he—wants to—and he—he take the
13 magazine and wants to—to see some pictures, and when
14 he didn't find anything, he put—the magazine in the—
15 in the box of—the second, but he didn't know that
16 the magazine is—it's uh—it's—the magazine it's
17 uh—that—the—teacher is the owner. And when—the
18 teacher finish—writing in the blackboard, he want—
19 he wants the magazine and he didn't find it. And by
20 (   ) the second student put the magazine in the box
21 of the first student.

In trying to tell a clear story to a listener who needed the information to complete a task, this learner used a variety of means to maintain clear reference to the various people and objects of central importance. He often repeated full noun phrases, and used a variety of modifiers to try to maintain clear reference. We would like to suggest that frequent use of articles and direct object pronouns in obligatory context in the narrative was a part of that attempt to maintain clear reference. Notice, for example, in lines 7–9, after the learner mentions 'pictures', and then uses the verb 'put', use of a direct object pronoun is necessary if the listener is not to make an incorrect interpretation; the learner uses a direct object pronoun 'it'—and then repeats the whole sentence using the full nominal 'magazine'. (Note the simultaneous erratic marking of the verb with *-ed*, *-s*, or *-ø*.)

What we are arguing here is that these learners used articles and direct object pronouns most accurately in the narrative because they realized (possibly unconsciously) that these features have an important function in maintaining a clear storyline. It may be that articles and direct object pronouns were supplied least often in the grammar test because cohesive ties are not required within a set of unconnected sentences; as the oral tasks required increasingly cohesive texts to be produced by the subjects, and applied increasing communicative pressure, the subjects increasingly supplied these two forms in obligatory contexts.

If indeed this explanation can account for the differential pattern of variable grammatical accuracy found between third person markers on the one hand, and articles and the direct object pronoun on the other hand, we must then conclude that the variable production of these learners was governed not by attention paid equally to all language forms, but to some degree by the nature of the discourse which the tasks required, and the sort of grammatical forms required by the discourse. As tasks elicit discourse which is increasingly cohesive and/or they apply increasing communicative pressure upon the speaker, some grammatical forms may improve in accuracy rate while others may decrease in accuracy.

The results of a study of this type provide some fairly clear guidelines to classroom teachers who wish to evaluate their learners' grammatical competence. Those familiar types of exercises involving sets of unconnected sentences which require the learner to produce or identify grammatically accurate forms, *as an end in itself*, will provide some insight into the learners' abilities. They may give an indication of how well the learner will cope, *in the classroom*, with those fill-in-the-blank or multiple-choice exercises commonly presented in grammar textbooks. If successful performance on such exercise types in class or in examinations is all that will be required of learners, then the needs analysis instruments may be limited to such form-oriented measures.

However, other exercise types, where the production of grammatically accurate forms serves an important discourse function, may provide a better indication of how well the learner will cope, *outside the classroom*, with the demands of interpersonal interaction or information-transfer situations. If learners' aims involve the ability to perform effectively in such situations, then the needs analysis instruments should incorporate such measures.

A very simple step in this direction would be for a teacher to avoid using fill-in-the-blank and multiple-choice formats to investigate learners' knowledge, particularly of grammatical forms that serve important cohesive and referential functions, like articles, pronouns, and demonstratives. What is needed for this purpose is measures like those in Appendices 2, 5, 6, and 7, which elicit longer stretches of discourse addressed to listeners who need to understand that discourse for some purpose.

In this section, we have illustrated the different kinds of pictures of learners' grammatical abilities which result from using different elicitation techniques. In Table 3.2 we summarize these techniques.

We are sure that classroom teachers and teachers-in-training will be able to think of analogous techniques which may be used (particularly with several tasks administered at the same point in time) to investigate other aspects of learners' grammatical competence in a second language and thereby increase our understanding of this complex, and highly variable, phenomenon.

Measures evaluating:	Type of measure	Examples
– learner language in terms of target language	discrete point test	multiple choice true/false fill-in-the-blank
	integrative test	cloze dictation
– learner language as an independent system	grammaticality judgments and making corrections	
	phonological	reading dialogues and word-lists
	syntactical and morphological	elicited imitation written sentence combining speaker-listener tasks* interviews and essays on set topics free oral/written production

* cf. Appendices 2, 5, 6, 7

Table 3.2   Elicitation techniques used in investigating learners'
grammatical competence

In the next chapter we move from a consideration of the sensitivity of learner language to differences in classroom tasks, to a broader consideration of the sociolinguistic aspect of the learner's competence.

8   Sociolinguistic competence

Mastery of sociolinguistic skills in a language entails mastery of speech act conventions, norms of stylistic appropriateness, and the uses of language to establish and maintain social relations.

It is interesting to note, at the outset, that research on the sociolinguistic abilities of second language learners has in large part been limited to the study of learners' mastery of certain speech acts in the target language. So, for example, the means learners use for encoding 'apology', 'gratitude', 'refusal', or 'compliment' in their second language have been studied by researchers. Relatively little attention has been devoted to other areas of second language learners' sociolinguistic competence, such as sensitivity to the norms associated with turn-taking in conversational interaction, the ability to use appropriate registers of the language, or the use of language variants to indicate social group membership or to mark relative status of members within a group.

Sociolinguists such as William Labov and social psychologists such as Howard Giles have pursued a broad program of research in areas such as these in their work with native speakers of various languages. Ethnographers have studied, in fine detail, the conventions of social interaction in specific cultures (cf. Bauman and Sherzer 1974). However, very little parallel work of this sort has been done in investigating the developing sociolinguistic competence of second language learners. We shall return to a consideration of how this sort of analysis might proceed later in this chapter.

'What would you say if ...'

The research which has been done on the developing ability of learners to perform speech acts in a second language has been very different from the parallel sort of research which has been done with native speakers, and which has already been described in part in Chapter 5. While, as we have seen, research on native speakers has involved the tape-recording and videotaping of actual communicative interactions and the analysis of these data in terms of speech acts and the linguistic forms used to realize them, research on second language learners has for the most part not looked at actual interactions involving learners. Rather, written 'role play' questionnaires have been used quite extensively to elicit speech act data in the study of learners. Typically, such questionnaires describe in a sentence or two a social situation, and then ask the learner to write a response. Here are two examples from Eisenstein and Bodman's (1986) study:

> Please read the following short descriptions of situations in which you might find yourself. Think of what *you* might say in response to this situation. Write your response (if any) in the space provided. Say as much or as little as you wish—you may choose to say nothing in several circumstances.
>
> 1. You board the bus, pay your money and take a seat near the front of the bus. Just before your stop, you signal the driver to stop. You move to the front, the bus comes to a stop, and the doors open.
> 2. It's your birthday, and you're having a few people over for dinner. A friend brings you a present. You unwrap it and find a blue sweater.
>
> (Eisenstein and Bodman 1986:179–80)

These researchers do, of course, ask native speakers to answer the same questionnaires to establish a baseline for comparison. But the relationship between any individual's performance on such questionnaires and their performance in actual oral interactions is as yet unclear. Researchers themselves have raised serious questions about the validity of this technique.

It would seem wise, in light of reservations such as these, for researchers to tape-record actual oral interactions among second language learners, and to analyze these in terms of particular speech acts and their linguistic realizations, and then to ask what in fact learners do and do not know in this area. Some studies, for example Bodman and Eisenstein (1988), are beginning to include such observational data.

Nevertheless, it is fair to say that most of the research on learners' ability to perform speech acts is based upon responses to questionnaires with items such as those above. And, when textbook writers have produced materials designed to teach second language learners to produce speech acts, if they have relied upon any research at all, it is this sort of questionnaire research which they have used. More often, as Richards (1984) has pointed out, the items selected are based on nothing more than the speculations of the materials writers.

On teaching speech acts

In recent years, language teachers have attempted to move away from the more limited goal of teaching only the grammatical forms of the language and have attempted to teach students to use the language communicatively. Research on pragmatics and sociolinguistics has broadened to include the investigation of the uses to which language is put, including the study of language functions, speech acts, and the like.

The initial reaction of curriculum developers and textbook writers was to organize the language-teaching syllabus around, for example, speech acts instead of grammatical points. Thus, instead of teaching students the present progressive tense of the verb, followed by the past progressive, followed by relative clauses, we began to teach students expressions used for complaints, followed by apologies, followed by invitations. The initial reaction, then, was to use the existing procedures for organizing a syllabus, and apply those procedures to a new content: speech acts.

During this initial phase, there was a great sense of excitement among language teachers at the prospect of being able to provide a more communicatively oriented syllabus, with commercially produced materials, to foster appropriate sociolinguistic skills among their learners. Despite this early enthusiasm, there now seems to be a general sense of disappointment with the types of materials which became available. It is worth considering why these materials might be failing to meet the high expectations created among practicing language teachers. Let us look at the exercises which accompany a unit titled 'Asking for Permission' in a textbook called *Communicate* (Morrow and Johnson 1979). In this unit, learners are introduced to the following four forms which are used to ask for permission in English:

1. Could I possibly come round into your garden?
2. Do you mind if I use your phone?
3. You don't mind if I smoke, do you?
4. I'd like to open the door. Does anyone mind?

To develop their ability to ask for permission, learners are then presented with the following exercise:

You have rented a room in Mrs Armstrong's house. Here are some things that you want to do. To be polite, you ask Mrs Armstrong first. You say ...

Could I possibly have a TV in my room?
Could I possibly put some pictures on the walls?
Could I possibly ask some friends to call round on Sunday?
Could I possibly get another front door key?
Could I possibly put my bicycle in the garage?
Could I possibly come back late on Saturday?
Could I possibly paint my bedroom?
Could I possibly move the furniture in my room?
Could I possibly use the washing machine?
Could I possibly dry my clothes on the line?

Now ask her permission in three other ways.

I'd like to ...

You don't mind if ...
Do you mind if...
(Morrow and Johnson 1979:76)

The most obvious point to make about these exercises is that they are essentially drills of the type more usually associated with audiolingual methodology. Consequently, they are hardly representative of the communicative use of language to accomplish a particular goal. Moreover, there is no indication given of when one or another of these ways of asking for permission might be more appropriate than the others. Finally, as several trainee language teachers have pointed out to us, the use of the expression *Could I possibly* ..., with its double modality, smacks of excessive politeness, almost to the point of sarcasm, especially in an American context. If learners really did go off and make frequent use of this expression for their polite requests, the Mrs Armstrongs of the world might eventually react rather unfavorably, or respond with the mysterious (to the learner): *Well, you possibly could, but not in my house!*

It is not our intention to denigrate the genuine attempts made by textbook writers to provide more functionally oriented materials of the type just illustrated. (In fact, we admire the honesty with which one of the *Communicate* authors describes the frustrations and the potential for absurdity which arose in his own attempts to create situations where examples of a structure could be practiced sufficiently but still count as authentic use; cf. Johnson 1983.) We simply wish to capture some of the reasons for the negative reactions that many language teachers have had to these materials. Essentially, the teachers' intuitions told them that there was something wrong. Indeed, as we have already argued in Chapter 2, language users, and that includes language teachers, experience the functional use of their language in probabilistic rather than categorial terms, as a phenomenon rooted in particular situations of use rather than a formal system abstracted away from social situations. Presentation of categorial systems of speech acts, only vaguely related to actual communicative situations, seemed wrong to teachers with this experience of language use.

And these teachers' intuitions were right. Research has since confirmed their impressions. In fact, what had happened was that textbook writers had gone from theory to materials either without doing empirical research, or else relying almost exclusively upon research of the questionnaire type described above to tell them what learners did and did not know about speech acts (never mind what they *needed* to know). In setting out to teach speech acts, they had committed the error of relying on speculation instead of detailed observation in deciding upon what it is the learners *need to learn* (Part Two above) and what it is the learners *know and do not know* already. We have examined some of the results of this research in Chapter 5; in two cases, teacher-researchers found that the speech acts and the forms used to realize them which were actually produced by native speakers in the target communicative situations were quite different from the speech acts taught to non-native speakers in popular communicative textbooks.

In short, the research which had been done on speech acts—both those performed by native speakers, and those known by learners—was inadequate when the goal was to produce communicative textbooks. The speech act approach is primarily strategic rather than sociolinguistic: that is, the focus is upon teaching students how to get a given general meaning across, with minimal attention paid either to sociolinguistic nuances, or to the implications of choosing, for example, a more formal or a less formal linguistic expression which might get the same general meaning across. It is not that textbooks in the 'functional' tradition *ignored* levels of formality; several of them provided lists of linguistic expressions labelled as more or less formal. The problem is that these labelled lists did not provide students with enough information to enable them to *use* the terms in context with any degree of confidence. If students had questions about when to use one linguistic expression as opposed to another, teachers were left to their own devices in providing directions and explanations. And, in *evaluating* their students' abilities to perform speech acts appropriately, teachers were also left to their own devices.

In fact, we need to know more about the sociolinguistic appropriacy of the various linguistic expressions used by learners to realize speech acts, and, if syllabuses are to be organized in terms of speech acts, we need to provide learners with more precise information about the social meaning inherent in their choice of one linguistic expression versus another to realize a particular speech act.

However, the 'speech act' approach itself, both in investigations of native speaker and learner behavior and in classroom presentation, is not the only approach to use in developing and evaluating the sociolinguistic competence of second language learners, and there is also some indication that it is not the best approach. Confirmation of this view can now be found in the theoretical literature, where much less attention is being devoted to the notion of speech acts. As Levinson (1983:278) has observed, 'there are some compelling reasons to think that speech act theory may slowly be superseded by much more complex multi-faceted pragmatic approaches to the functions utterances perform'. It has become clear that what has to be taken into account in determining the function or purpose of utterances is tied to the general context and the nature of the interaction in which those utterances actually occur. It is to this area of investigation that we now turn.

1 Investigating learners' sociolinguistic skills

In the previous section, we suggested that much needs to be learned about the sociolinguistic skills of second language learners, in areas other than their ability to perform speech acts in the target language. Rivers (1983:25) describes the language learner's need for sociolinguistic competence this way: '[Students] need to understand how language is used in relation to the structure of society and its patterns of inner and outer relationships, if they are to avoid clashes, misunderstandings, and hurt.'

Thus, if we are to analyze the sociolinguistic competence of second language learners, we must step back from a narrow focus on the linguistic forms used in speech acts and ask, what happens to people's language when they interact socially? Other interesting areas for investigation might include the study of learners' acquisition of turn-taking skills in spoken interaction (as in, for example, business meetings or academic discussions), or their mastery of the norms associated with particular registers of the target language (registers appropriate to, for example, doctor–patient office interviews, or graduate student–professor office meetings). Teachers of the spoken language may often informally note that their students have difficulty in areas such as these—and students themselves are typically quite interested in understanding the social dimension of language use in such areas.

Taking turns

Smith (1986), teaching advanced speaking skills in English to university students, noticed that these language learners had a great deal of difficulty functioning well in university courses when they were required to interact in small groups using the language. She became particularly interested in assessing her students' abilities to handle the dynamics of turn-taking in these academic discussions. She found very little in the research literature on second language learners to help her; most studies on oral skills had concentrated on lecture presentation and comprehension rather than on interactive language use. She turned to the broader literature on conversational organization, which pointed out that conversation is distinguished from other oral modes like lecture and narrative in that:

1. The participants take turns, exchanging the roles of speaker and hearer.
2. The exchange is not automatic, that is, the parties *do* something to accomplish the exchange.
3. The order and length of turns is not predetermined.

4. Theoretically, the allocation of turns is the responsibility of all participants.
(McLaughlin 1984:91)

In a typical conversation, there may be simultaneous speech, 'back-channel commentary' (i.e. the 'uh-huh's, 'right's, and other comments that show that one is listening), pauses of varying lengths, and differences in nonverbal behavior between speaker and hearer. From a review of the ethnographic literature, Smith learned that cultures differ to a great degree in the 'rules' governing the use of all these phenomena in conversation, and she found evidence in one study (Scarcella 1983) that Spanish speakers transfer their 'rules' for back-channel commentary into English conversations. Smith speculated that at least some of her students might be transferring inappropriate turn-taking systems into their English conversations and academic discussions, and decided to analyze one of the discussions which had taken place among the students in her spoken English class.

As is usual in many spoken English classes, Smith's students had been given an assignment requiring them to prepare for, and participate in, a small-group discussion on a given topic. In this case, three students (a Japanese male (Alpha), a Vietnamese male (Beta), and a Chinese female (Gamma), sat around a table in front of their fellow students and conducted a discussion on the classroom behavior of US university students. They had been given a week and a half to prepare for the content of their discussion; they had constructed a questionnaire (with questions like 'How often do you study until midnight?'), administered it to native speakers, pooled the data, and made comparisons with behavior in their own countries. They were now reporting their conclusions to the class. They had not been given any guidance on discussion techniques 'other than an admonition to make certain that everyone talked'. The discussion lasted about nine and a half minutes, with the first three minutes devoted to reporting on the information gathered, and the remaining six and a half minutes consisting of a comparison with behavior in the students' native countries and the expression of opinion about the relative merits of the various systems. Smith video-taped the discussion and then transcribed it. (The discussion in Smith (1986) of the transcription conventions adopted and issues which affected the transcription would be useful for those interested in using this technique and with the time to use it.) She found that learners Alpha and Gamma seemed to have the least difficulty with turn-taking; they spoke the most (about four minutes apiece), used back-channel commentary and pausing appropriately, and used appropriate nonverbals. Beta, on the other hand, had a great deal of difficulty with turn-taking. Although he was prepared for the discussion, he spoke relatively little. He took only two long turns, both initiated in response to direct questions put to him by Alpha. He used back-channel commentary only once in the entire discussion. He maintained eye contact primarily with his notes, missing at least one opportunity to speak when Gamma directed a question to him, and he failed to notice her gaze which was focussed on him. With all three speakers, there was a lack of cohesion between some adjacent turns. Smith points out that all three came from cultures in which indirection (and a corollary lack of explicit marking of cohesive ties between turns) is tolerated more than in the American culture. The learners' performance on their oral discussion task indicated to Smith that at least some learners were inappropriately transferring interactional patterns from their native language and culture to interactions in the second language. The results of this investigation evidence a need for explicit presentation and practice on turn-taking norms in American English, since these learners had not unconsciously absorbed the appropriate norms from their contact with American academic society.

An important point about Smith's study is that, although the transcription of the conversation of these three learners was extremely time-consuming, it resulted in the sort of material which can be used in a great many ways. The teacher can return to the data for a variety of purposes: Smith herself went back to it to look at the linguistic expressions used by her students to express opinions. Other aspects of these learners' interlanguage can be analyzed as well, once the data are gathered and tabulated in transcribed form: grammatical, sociolinguistic, and strategic skills can be analyzed, and the learners' own language used as examples in pedagogical presentations on problem areas identified in this way.

Have we got the right script?

Another sort of analysis of the learners' sociolinguistic skills—and one which is far less time-consuming than that used in Smith's study—might focus on their mastery of the norms appropriate to communicative activities which are common in the culture. Ranney (1986) became interested in her students' abilities to function well in medical consultations in the doctor's office. She was particularly interested in learners' perceptions of the social situation and norms for that situation.

Such norms are not always inferrable from the speech acts learners perform. Ranney cites Olshtain's (1983) study, in which Russian subjects were given a questionnaire describing a situation in which one forgets to attend a meeting with one's boss. When asked what verbal response they would provide in such a situation, the Russian subjects listed very few apologies. One might infer from these verbal responses that the subjects did not consider the described infraction to be very serious. However, when the subjects were later asked directly about the situation, they stated that they considered it to be so highly unacceptable to miss a meeting with one's boss that they couldn't imagine what they would say in such a situation. Ranney suggests that an alternative to the speech act approach in investigating learners' sociolinguistic competence might be the direct examination of the learners' rules and norms for the use of speech which are tied to particular events such as the medical consultation.

The notion of 'scripts', developed by Schank and Abelson (1977) is helpful here. In research on scripts, individuals are asked to list the actions that typically take place in a given situation. Such a 'script' encodes an individual's knowledge of the actions taken in a culturally stereotypic situation; every individual has hundreds of scripts for such events as catching a bus, going grocery shopping, asking the time, and so on. Further, such scripts may vary from one culture to another. This technique is a simple one, easily usable by classroom teachers.

Ranney asked four Japanese and four American subjects to write out scripts for a visit to the doctor's office. The Americans expected the following general sequence: check in with the receptionist, sit and wait, read magazines, be called by the nurse, be tested by the nurse, wait for the doctor, talk to the doctor, be examined by the doctor, receive advice regarding treatment, and leave. The Japanese script followed the same general pattern, but with the following exceptions: the nurse was more often expected to see the patient after the doctor than before, and to play the role of explaining medication rather than giving pre-consultation tests. Further, all the Japanese subjects agreed that receiving medication was part of the script, whereas only some American subjects mentioned this.

A questionnaire administered to all the subjects confirmed the differences between the Japanese and American subjects. For example, the Japanese agreed more often than the Americans with a statement that medication should always be given, and all the Japanese agreed that doctors always ask about any information they need to make a diagnosis, while the Americans felt that doctors do this only sometimes.

What patterns of communication might we expect, based on these norms? Ranney concludes that since all the subjects agreed that doctors have high status, all will probably be trying to use a formal register. Since all the subjects expect to answer the doctor's questions on symptoms, all will be trying to perform the speech act of giving information. The Japanese patients may expect nurses to perform different actions and speech acts than do the American patients, and if these do not occur, they may request nurses to provide them. If the Japanese subjects are not given medication, they may want to make a request for it. Since the Americans do not believe that doctors automatically ask for the information they need to make a diagnosis, they may be more likely than the Japanese to volunteer information that is not directly requested.

The focus upon culturally important communicative situations, and the elicitation of learners' (and native speakers') scripts for these, seems to us to provide the language teacher with easily obtainable and valuable information, useful in the teaching of sociolinguistic skills. What, for example, are the learners' scripts for a college lecture class? for a service encounter? for a transaction with a bank teller? And how do these differ from the scripts of native speakers of the language?

The needs analyses which we have just discussed have been provided simply as examples of the sort of measures of sociolinguistic skills which can be usefully carried out by classroom teachers. An investigation of the expectations and scripts of language learners with regard to the social norms relating to interactions in particular settings can be very helpful to the classroom teacher in deciding how to help students develop sociolinguistic skills in the language. The observation and transcription of learners' oral interactions—while undoubtedly very time-consuming—can provide valuable data, which can be analyzed in terms of speech acts, or turn-taking skills, or social appropriacy of the linguistic expressions used. Such transcriptions can also be useful in teaching sociolinguistic skills. Since it is our belief that effective techniques for needs analysis are usually also effective for *teaching* in the classroom, we now turn to a consideration of the means of teaching those skills.

2 An alternative approach

In the previous section, we have suggested that a different way of looking at sociolinguistic competence is not to regard it as a set of lists of speech acts, or as lists of any type, but rather to view it as part of an individual's knowledge of the nature of social interaction in a particular culture. An alternative approach to the teaching of speech acts is based on the assumption that we cannot 'discrete-point' teach sociolinguistic competence. A knowledge of appropriate conditions for language use must involve an understanding of the way in which such factors as the roles of the speaker, hearer, and overhearer *interact* with the communicative setting, the topic of discourse, and the purposes of the participants. Whatever approach we use to teach sociolinguistic competence must then be integrative in nature, with the goal of our approach to sensitize learners to the social diversity of language, rather than to teach them long lists of discrete phrases.

How is the teacher to do this? What should the syllabus consist of when the goal is the improvement of sociolinguistic competence? In other words, what is the language teacher to teach?

We would like to suggest that in helping language students to attain sociolinguistic competence, the language teacher in fact should *not* follow a structured, discrete-point syllabus. Much more appropriate would be the use of a problem-solving, task-based approach similar to the interactive learning approach described by Heath (1986). In this approach, learners are asked to tape-record their own language habits and those of their friends, family, fellow workers, shopkeepers, and so on. These language data (obviously useful for needs analysis) are then used in class for discussion. Although students may bring up anything they want to discuss, the focus of the discussion is usually upon language as an instrument of social interaction. The language itself becomes both the focus and the medium of the class discussion. The learners are experts here: only they know who the speakers were and what the outcome of the recorded interaction was. The teacher, and at times outside linguistic consultants, are authorities who help to interpret the contents of the tape itself. According to Heath, this approach has been used successfully with ESL learners at Roxbury Community College in Boston.

Fostering interactive learning

What we propose here is that language learners as a group be asked to solve problems posed by a consideration of language in use in actual communicative situations. A descriptive framework might be proposed by the teacher (or by an outside resource person, as Heath suggests) to encourage them to reflect upon specific aspects of the social uses of language within each particular communicative situation. Such an approach, we would like to argue, provides the integrative element which the development of sociolinguistic competence necessarily requires.

We should also like to emphasize the essentially 'local' nature of this approach. The data which enters into classroom consideration and use has not been chosen by some distant textbook writer speculating on what people say to each other, but is typically selected by the learners themselves as a sample of what linguistic and social demands will be placed on them as users of the second language in the settings which they identify as relevant. As such, these data are effective both for needs analysis and for instruction. What the teacher can offer is guidance and practical assistance, as an experienced informant, on how to approach the 'natives', how to prepare the elicitation procedures in advance, how to identify a particular local social event, and, in general, provision of the kind of support that enables the learners to create their own learning experiences. This type of approach puts the learner who does not know what the 'natives' actually say (in a particular sociocultural setting) in the same position as the ethnographer wishing to gain an accurate picture of what typically happens in different kinds of speech events. An inevitable part of this approach is the crucial experience of interaction with fluent speakers of the language. If the learner, as ethnographer, brings observations or data back to the classroom to share with other learners, it is that learner who assumes some responsibility for knowing what took place. In this way, we have gone a long way towards reaping the general benefits of fostering 'learner-centered' classroom activities.

The four components

In the typical 'lesson plan' which we would like to suggest here, four basic components would be used:

1. Plan for interaction
2. Interact
3. Transcribe interaction
4. Reflect

In the 'plan for interaction' portion of the lesson, the teacher helps the student select social situations and speech events which are problematic for them, and which they wish to study in more depth. The teacher helps the students both to identify local social events of interest, and to prepare elicitation materials or procedures. For example, university students may decide that they are interested in learning more about appropriate speech behavior in the classroom. The teacher may help them to select particular contexts in which to tape (and, if necessary, to obtain permission to tape), or to prepare a set of interview questions to address to native speakers, both students and teachers. The teacher may be able to provide the students with audio- or video-tapes of actual interactions among native speakers in the classroom, which may then be studied. Alternatively, students may decide that they are interested in looking at service encounters. The teacher may help them to select a particular context and content; the students may then decide to prepare questionnaires, to elicit 'scripts', or even to observe native speakers in service encounters directly, either 'live' or role-played. Clearly, the teacher will need to help the students to prepare: in constructing questionnaires, in eliciting 'scripts', in framing hypotheses about sociolinguistic norms which they expect to hold in the target situations, and possibly in obtaining tapes of native speaker interactions in those situations. Such preparation is crucial if all the students are to gain the most from the next part of the lesson.

In the 'interact' portion of a lesson, learners might be asked to tape-record native speakers, or tape-record themselves *and* native speakers in various interactions in the target culture—in service encounters, seminars, parties, office interactions, to name only a few. (Examples of the procedure are presented in Appendix 4). Variations on this basic procedure might be used in an EFL setting, using role play and media like television or radio where possible. For example, learners might tape-record situation comedies or advertisements in which native speakers interact, and examine the use of language in these.

In the 'transcribe' part of the lesson, tape-recordings are brought to class and the whole class transcribes them. A useful (though not necessarily sociolinguistic) by-product here is that the transcription process itself is likely to provide very interesting and important 'learning opportunities' (cf. Allwright 1986), as students may perceive different bits of language differently and have to negotiate among themselves to decide how to transcribe them. The transcription agreed upon is copied and distributed to the class.

Finally, in the 'reflect' part of the lesson, the learners as a group look at what is being accomplished by the language in terms of social interaction. Questions to be asked about the data might be:

What are the roles of the participants here?
Who has the highest status?
For whose benefit is each utterance?
What, in the lexicon, grammar, or phonology, gives you clues to the answers to these questions?
Are the interactants 'converging' or 'diverging' (see below)?

As these questions are asked about a variety of different sorts of recorded interactions (for example, in formal or informal settings; with interactants in a variety of roles such as boss and secretary, professor and student, salesman and customer), the learners' sociolinguistic competence should benefit.

Frameworks for reflection

The teacher might usefully provide the students with a descriptive framework to be used in the 'reflect' portion of the lesson, if the learners are not used to considering language from this perspective and need some guidelines. One type of framework can be based on what has been described as 'a resource which is commonly overlooked in listening comprehension ... the voice of the speaker' (Brown and Yule 1983:76). Upon reflection, it is often possible to determine a number of characteristics of particular speakers, simply by devoting some attention to their voices. How old is this speaker, what sex, and what level of education? Is he or she American or British, or even from a more specific geographical area; self-confident or shy; friendly or not; casual or formal, and so on. After all, when listening to radio programs, native speakers of a language often use this type of unconscious characterization process to make decisions about what kind of person (with what kinds of attitudes) they are listening to. And such characterizations are often culturally determined. In the initial stages the teacher, as the local informant among the classroom group, may be the most reliable judge of which impressions produced by the learners are probably most accurate. Yet, as learners develop a better awareness of the relationship between speaker's voice and speaker characteristics, they will develop a useful sensitivity to a range of socially relevant factors concerning the people they're talking to.

Another type of descriptive framework might be based upon Speech Accommodation Theory (SAT), a current model for the analysis of sociolinguistic interaction. In this model, the notions of 'convergence' and 'divergence' are central to the understanding of the role of language in social interaction. Basically, SAT predicts that speakers will try to converge linguistically (that is, produce language which moves closer in form) toward the speech patterns they believe to be characteristic of their listeners when they desire the social approval of the listeners and when the social costs of linguistic convergence are not too high. Speakers will fail to converge, or even diverge, linguistically from those believed characteristics of their listeners when they define the interaction in intergroup terms and desire to emphasize their own group membership in contrast to the group membership of the listener.

Any communicative encounter may be described in terms of convergence and divergence. We may look at any such encounter and ask: Are the participants converging or diverging? How do we know (i.e. what are the linguistic variants that we are using to make that decision)? What social group membership is signalled by the particular linguistic variants used by the speaker? And so on.

This framework has been used by researchers to look at sociolinguistic competence in a variety of contexts. For example, Rampton's (1987) analysis of interaction in a language classroom is very interesting for the language teacher to consider. Rampton describes the way in which Pakistani learners of English in Britain used a distinctively Pakistani-English linguistic form (*me no*) in addressing their English teacher, when in fact they were perfectly capable of using the more standard *I don't*. The reason for their deliberate divergence from standard English, Rampton argues, was their desire to identify themselves with the Pakistani community in Britain rather than with the English teacher's reference group.

The SAT framework is a useful one for enabling the teacher to sensitize learners to the sorts of linguistic variation which occur in the target culture, and possibly in their own language classroom. It is an approach which goes beyond the narrow focus upon speech acts which we mentioned above as a seeming limitation of current research on the sociolinguistic competence of second-language learners. It permits researchers and teachers to focus upon all kinds of sociolinguistic phenomena—including the uses of all aspects of language, phonological and syntactic forms as well as speech acts—to mark group membership and status within the group, convergence as well as divergence.

Because the knowledge which must be mastered (that is, sociolinguistic competence) is so complex, and because so much of it operates below the level of consciousness, we have argued that it is best taught indirectly, by integrative rather than discrete-point means, and that a task-based, problem-solving approach offers a promising way of doing this. Our proposals in this area have concentrated on what is possible in an ESL situation, where the learner has regular access to the target culture. In the foreign language learning situation, where there may be extremely limited opportunities to take part in everyday interactional events characteristic of the target culture, the use of task-based, problem-solving activities will nevertheless create opportunities to develop the organizing and negotiating aspects of interactional language use. Reports from the Bangalore Project (Johnson 1982; Brumfit 1984; Beretta and Davies 1985; Prabhu 1987) indicate that a syllabus organized around problem-solving tasks and feedback can effectively accomplish, and in many respects improve on, what a traditional linguistic syllabus provides. A similar approach has been advocated in terms of 'scenarios', with the four stages of 'preparation—rehearsal—performance—debriefing', specifically proposed for developing interactive skills in the foreign language classroom. This approach is described in detail in Di Pietro (1987).

In the next chapter we move from a consideration of the development of the learner's skills in the social and interactional uses of language to the development of the transactional aspect of language use; we turn to the evaluation and development of strategic competence in the second language learner.

9 Strategic competence

Mastery of strategic skills in a language entails the ability to transmit information to a listener and correctly interpret information received, and includes the mastery of communication strategies, used to deal with problems which may arise in the transmission of this information. Strategic competence, then, has to do with the ability to successfully get one's meaning across to particular listeners.

Our knowledge about the strategic competence of second language learners is still incomplete. Two broad areas relate to strategic competence: (1) the overall skill of a learner in successfully transmitting information to a listener, or interpreting information transmitted, and (2) the use of communication strategies by a speaker or listener when problems arise in the process of transmitting information. As far as we know, very little attempt has been made to investigate the first area, the learner's overall skills in strategic competence. Some systematic research of this kind has been done with native speakers of English, studying their 'transactional speech'—instances where the speaker is primarily concerned with transmitting information to a listener. Because we feel that this research provides a model for analysis of the overall strategic competence of second language learners, we will describe its general principles here.

Research with native speakers (Yule 1982; Brown and Yule 1983; Brown *et al.* 1984) developed a task-based methodology for the objective evaluation of the communicative effectiveness of English native-speaker adolescents in using the spoken language. In this methodology, a series of transactional language tasks (narrative, descriptive, and instructional) was developed, in which a speaker had to transfer information to a listener who required this information in order to complete some task. The aim was to set up a situation in which the speaker alone was in possession of the relevant knowledge, and where the speaker knew the listener needed that information in order to complete a task. The problem for the speaker, then, is to determine which aspects of the information that he or she possesses are relevant to the task at hand and to control the flow of information to the listener so that the listener is provided with the relevant information (and not credited with knowledge which he or she could not possibly be expected to have). In studies with native speakers, this methodology elicited spontaneous speech from the subjects, but at the same time allowed the researchers to determine what the essential content of that speech should be. An objective scoring procedure was then developed and applied to speaker performances, so that speakers could be compared with one another with regard to their degree of success in communicating the essential information required by the task. We have found this research technique to be quite successful in evaluating the overall transactional effectiveness of second language learners as well as in eliciting the use of communication strategies, which we will now describe.

The second area of strategic competence, the use of communication strategies to solve problems encountered in the transmission of information, has been investigated by many researchers. Speakers use communication strategies when the following conditions occur:

1. a speaker desires to communicate a meaning x to a listener, *and*
2. the speaker believes the language form he or she wants to use to communicate meaning x cannot be produced, *and*
3. the speaker chooses to:
   (a) avoid (not attempt to communicate meaning x), *or*
   (b) attempt alternate means to communicate meaning x such as mime, word coinage, circumlocution, etc. (The speaker stops trying alternatives when it seems to him or her that there is shared meaning.)

A great deal of research has been published on learners' use of communication strategies in situations where message transmission is impeded in some way; we provide references to some of this work at the end of Part Three.

1 Using a task-based methodology

In our attempts to study the strategic competence of second language learners, we have applied the principles of the task-based methodology described earlier to the second language learning context. The aim of the task-based procedure is to provide a speaker with some information to convey, a listener who requires that information, and an awareness that an information gap exists.

In our study (Tarone and Yule 1987), we worked with twenty-four learners of English as a second language and nine native speakers of English. Two learners participated in each session, one South American and one Asian; the only language they shared was English. One learner was given the speaker role and the other was asked to be the listener. Both learners were given tasks. The speaker was required to look at a set of visual stimuli presented on a video screen which the listener could not see, and to verbally transmit to the listener information he or she perceived on the screen. There were three separate tasks which, for the speaker, were as follows: (1) to describe four objects which appeared one after the other; (2) to give instructions for the assembly of an apparatus, and (3) to narrate a story reporting actions taking place in a classroom scene. The speaker knew he or she was going to be tape-recorded and sat face to face with the listener across a table divided by a low screen. The speaker was allowed as much time as was needed to complete each task. To accompany each visual stimulus shown on the screen to the speaker, the listener had a set of still photographs, marked A, B, and C. In the description task, for instance, the listener had a still photograph of the hairbrush which appeared on the TV screen, labelled B, plus two other still photographs, A and C, of two other types of brush (see Appendix 5 for similar examples). The listener's task was to listen to the speaker's message and identify which of the three photographs best fit the description. The speaker could see the listener's face and upper body (though not the still photographs the listener was working with). After the speaker had finished all the tasks, the listener and speaker changed places—the listener becoming the speaker on a new round of tasks of the same type, and the speaker becoming the listener. The speaker's utterances were tape-recorded and transcribed.

The same procedure was followed in gathering data from nine native speakers of English.

An analysis of all the transcriptions was then performed.

'The three legs'

To illustrate some typical ways in which these speakers performed their strategic competence, let us now consider the three entities featured in Figure 3.3 overleaf (the legs of a Christmas tree stand), and the ways in which a group of individuals, both native speakers and non-native speakers of English, referred to these in our study (Table 3.3 overleaf) as they were instructing a listener in the proper procedure to be used in assembling an apparatus.

As may be seen, a great deal of variability occurred in the linguistic means used by both native and non-native speakers of English to realize this act of reference or, indeed, any of the others elicited in our study. We believe that this is because strategic competence involves the ability to select an *effective* means of performing a communicative act, as in referring to an entity, one which enables a particular listener to identify the intended referent. Thus, strategic competence is gauged, not by degree of correctness (as with grammatical competence) but rather by degree of success, or effectiveness. Clearly, individuals may be able to successfully communicate their intended meanings without necessarily demonstrating accuracy in the linguistic form of the target language. Further, different linguistic forms may prove to be successful under different circumstances, with different listeners.

Figure 3.3 'The three legs'

Native speaker	1:	three metal pieces about this long . . . about this wide (gesturing with hands)
	2:	three sticks or bars that are metal that are curved
	3:	the three legs
	4:	three legs
	5:	three metal pieces which become the legs
Non-native speaker	6:	three same pieces are the [hit] or you can say the feet
	7:	(mumble) has a legs (mumble)
	8:	three large objects ( ) to sustain the round object
	9:	three long things ( ) they has a special they have a special shape
	10:	one part of this object ( ) are going to use like legs
	11:	three things three metallic like a lengs(?)
	12:	(no response)
	13:	three legs
	14:	three legs
	15:	three pieces of flat and just curved . . . plates . . . three I think it is made of metal
	16:	a three leg
	17:	three legs . . . like round leg . . three round legs
	18:	three [legɪz] which is curved
	19:	a half inch side and then six inch long shape or strips I think made out of [stirz] . . . a three strips
	20:	three long things ( ) from metal about ten centimeter each
	21:	some kind of metal . . . a metal piece which was long and thin

Table 3.3 Describing the Christmas tree stand

In fact, we believe that the *range* of expressions available to any individual, whether learner or native speaker, will prove to be dependent upon a minimum of three factors: (1) the speaker's knowledge of the language; (2) the speaker's knowledge of the world, and (3) the speaker's assessment of the listener's knowledge of the world and the language. For example, professional mechanics, whether native speakers or learners, have specialized knowledge about engine parts which will allow them to refer to those parts far more effectively than those of us who are not familiar with the inner workings of engines. Where the listener shares this knowledge, the mechanic's effectiveness in referring to engine parts must surely be relatively high; where the listener does not share this knowledge, the range of expressions available to the mechanic which are likely to be effective must surely be greatly reduced. And the range must be further reduced when one or another of the interlocutors does not have adequate mastery of the language itself, and thus does not know the relevant linguistic expressions, whatever his or her level of knowledge of the field.

Let us return to a consideration of the linguistic expressions which were used in our study to refer to the shaded entities in Figure 3.3. In some cases simple nominals were used (for example 'three legs', 'three long things') but in other cases a range of more complex nominal expressions was used (for example 'three metal pieces which become the legs', 'three large objects (   ) to sustain the round object'). It is important to observe that, while the native speakers employed one range of referring expressions, and the non-native speakers employed another, those ranges overlapped. Some types of expressions were used by both groups, while other types seem to have been used only by the native speaker group, or only by the non-native speakers.

One difference between native and non-native speakers seems to develop in the degree of specificity, or level of detail, required in the encoding of the message. We see this pattern, not just in Table 3.3, but throughout our data. In deciding what to include and what to leave out of a message, there seems to be a level of detail which members of the native speaker group often generally agree upon. Members of the non-native speaker group may provide either more, or less, detail than members of the native speaker group.

The strategy of 'over-elaboration', where non-native speakers included more detail than the native speaker group did, occurred often in our study. Here, in the interest of successful communication, learners seem to attempt to build in redundancy, to send a bigger signal, perhaps to ensure that the basic message does get across. (A similar phenomenon is described as 'over-informativeness' by Blum-Kulka and Olshtain (1986) who account for it in terms of the learners' general lack of confidence in their communicative competence. These writers go on to suggest that learners operate with a motto of the following type: 'The less confident you are that you can get the meaning across, the more words and contextual information you use' (1986:176).)

'The arm of the chair is … when you use for to write'

One beneficial effect of this strategy may be that the listener is provided with extra opportunities to identify the intended referent or action. One detrimental effect may be that the main point of the message becomes obscured, or the listener gets distracted, by the elaborate description of some minor element in the scenario. If we are concerned with what the learners do or do not know, then we should concentrate our attention (and, ultimately, the learner's attention too) on what native speakers typically do in such situations. Here are some examples of how our two groups went about identifying a tablet armchair (which had a fairly minor circumstantial role) in the course of a narrative (see Appendix 7 'The magazine story').

Figure 3.4   The tablet armchair

Native speaker	1:	her desk
	2:	one of the front, desks
	3:	on her . . .on her, ah, desk
	4:	her desk
	5:	where that girl was sitting
Non-native speaker	6:	the . . . chair
	7:	the little table but eh what is the name of . . . the . . . in his chair
	8:	her table
	9:	a . . . chair. a desk
	10:	the arm, of the chair. the arm of the chair is when the, when you use for to write

Table 3.4   Referring to a tablet armchair

A good example of over-elaboration is Speaker **10**'s extended definition 'the arm of the chair is . . . when you use for to write'. Note that none of the native speaker group bothered to try to specify that this was a particular type of chair. Rather, in this case, there seems to be some agreement on the part of the native speakers as to the level of detail necessary to identify this referent. The operating assumption may be that the more linguistic material devoted to the identification of an entity, the more significant that entity must be in the course of events being described.

Of course, there are also cases where the non-native speaker group provided less detail than the native speakers. In another task (see

Appendix 6 'Making coffee'), in referring to some hot water being poured from a container, for example, the group of native speakers of English all mentioned both the water *and* the container, while all the non-native speakers mentioned *only* the water and *not* the container. Of these two options, over- and under-elaboration, it is probably better for learners to err on the side of the former, in the initial stages, in order to achieve greater success in terms of information transfer.

2 Communication strategies

We may assume that, in some cases, the speakers encountered a problem in referring to these entities. Some seem to have been searching for a more precise nominal expression than the one they ended up producing; we presume this in some cases because of hesitation on the part of the speaker either before or after the use of the term (for example 'three long things (   )', and 'three pieces of flat and just curved ... plates ...'), or because, as with Speaker 7 in Table 3.4, the learner tells us of difficulty in accessing the desired expression. In other cases, learners may encounter difficulties in communicating because of poor pronunciation. In the research literature, the linguistic (and in some cases non-linguistic) signals used by such speakers in place of the linguistic expression which they desire to use have been referred to as 'communication strategies'.

It is hard for the observer to tell, just by looking at the data in Tables 3.3 and 3.4, whether any given speaker is using a communication strategy or not—that is, whether the expression produced is precisely the one the speaker desires, or whether it is a substitute for some other more precise expression which the speaker would prefer to use under other circumstances.

One way of establishing whether communication strategies have been used because of some lack of linguistic resources on the part of second language learners is to ask the speakers, after performing the task, whether the referential expressions used were in fact acceptable to them in communicating their intended meanings; this approach is fraught with problems, among them lapses of memory on the part of the speaker, and the whole issue of speaker consciousness in using such strategies. It is at times useful to ask the learner to perform the same task in both the native and the second languages, tape-recording and comparing the performances in the two languages in order to gain a preliminary idea of data points where a more precise linguistic expression is used in the native language but not in the second language. Clearly, this procedure is more easily undertaken by the researcher than by the practicing teacher.

Another approach, useful for the second language teacher, is to simply avoid making any distinction at all between communication strategies and other sorts of expressions, but to note that there are simple and more complex expressions, and more or less effective ones, and to observe any differences between native and non-native speakers in the way they perform the same tasks. Where differences are observed, there may be valuable teaching points to be found.

One of the teacher's goals is to provide students with the linguistic resources they need to be effective in performing communicative acts such as the act of reference. The pedagogical goal must therefore be to teach students not only those simple nominal expressions which they are likely to need in referring to entities in particular areas of knowledge (for example, the terms for items of equipment in a university physics laboratory to students who are engineering majors) but also to equip them with the linguistic resources they need to use communication strategies—for example, to construct more complex nominals when they do not know the desired simpler expression. We would hope to provide students with enough of these linguistic resources so that they can perform communicative tasks with the same degree of success as reasonably competent native speakers. What teachers want to avoid is clearly dysfunctional behavior on the part of non-native speakers—such as the behavior of Speaker 12 in Table 3.3—an abandonment of the attempt to refer to the entity at all when the speaker 'does not know the word for it'.

Another common dysfunctional strategy, described by Nelson (1989), is the learner's insistence on *repeating* (often useful only as a *first* strategy), instead of employing the more effective strategies of elaboration. This may happen when the learner *does* know the right word, as in the following exchange:

Learner: I'm looking for [təstəl].
E.N.:   Erica Tesdell? Her office is 110.
Learner: [təstəl]
E.N.:   A woman teacher?
Learner: No, man. [təstəl]
E.N.:   What does he look like?
          etc.
(Nelson 1989)

The learner finally found him: Ted Taylor. In this case, the learner knew the name, but was unable to communicate it easily because of poor pronunciation and the inability to use strategies other than repetition. More effective strategies had to come from the listener.

In spite of the difficulties involved in defining the phenomenon precisely, there is no doubt that the following situation occurs frequently in the experience of any speaker, but most frequently in the attempt to communicate in a foreign language: a problem is encountered in the attempt, for example, to refer to some entity, and the speaker resorts to alternative strategies for communicating his or her meaning.

Several of the types of communication strategy previously reported in the literature could be observed in the interactions which occurred in our study. We exemplify these here, as a means of illustrating the nature of communication strategies. (For a very detailed taxonomy of types of communication strategies, see Paribakht 1982.)

Circumlocution, in which the speaker describes the properties of the target object or action (i.e. its color, size, shape, function, etc.), occurred in learner accounts such as these:

J5: The color is, uh, dark, and uh ... the size is just uh, uh, as a hand ... it is made of uh, la, leather

K5: OK this is oval shape one side has a hair and the backside has string in middle part so you can put your fing—your hands.

S1: It is made by rubber—but it is cutted on front—that you can have your fingers out—if you wear that

Approximation, in which the speaker uses a term which shares a number of semantic features with the target lexical item or structure, occurred in this sort of learner account:

S8: Maybe is something like a rope (describing an electrical cord)

J6: And the shape is like a octopus (laugh) but it has just three legs. Not eight legs. Head, and, three legs. Like octopus. (laugh) (describing a Christmas tree stand)

It is interesting to note that, in their use of approximation, the learners in general seemed to try to avoid 'culture-specific' analogies—as below, when S8 attempted and then abandoned an analogy of *set screws* to *sardine can keys*, apparently because he decided half-way through that his listener could not be expected to know what a sardine can key was:

S8: we have three key, three, three objects that, li like a key, when you open a sardines? Mm, no, no, no, no, no. Forget that (laugh) we are going to confuse that.

Speakers did seem to take the identity of the listener into account in selecting communication strategies, and seemed to operate with definite hypotheses about the sorts of culturally based information which the listener could be expected to have at his or her disposal. Here, the speaker's assessment of the listener's knowledge had an obvious effect upon the strategies employed.

Literal translation, or word-for-word translation from the native language, was used by some learners, though relatively infrequently. We were surprised to find this at all, as the success of this strategy must depend upon the speaker's assumption that either the listener knows his or her native language (which, in our study, was clearly not the case), or that the speaker's native language and English are similar enough in structure for literal translation from the native language to produce a successful communication (one never knows whether a communication strategy will be successful until it is tried). An example of the use of an apparent literal translation is:

S5:   In each, in each extreme [Spanish *extremo* = English *end*], in each uh ... is an English word, *extreme*? (laugh) has something for connecting, on the equipment.

Mime, or the use of nonverbal means of communicating, seemed to be used fairly frequently in these interactions by most learners. Two types of mime occurred, in fact; in one case, mime took the place of a desired form, as in:

S6:   the oval is the big one and the other part is what, take to (demonstrates holding the handle of a brush)
7A: (who who cuts)—uh—who can uh—like this.

More frequently, mime accompanied the speaker's use of another communication strategy, as below where the speaker uses circumlocution and mime simultaneously:

J5:   And the shape is, the big, down part is just like, this and uh, this size, and the upper side is just like this.

Message abandonment, in which the speaker starts out using communication strategies but then gives up and stops talking, also occurred in these interactions:

C4:   I saw I saw the TV the first you—eh—eh—[lak] put together and you—do the next—step—I can't (mumble) it I'm sorry.
S3:   crush or to—oh I don't know the (mumble)—I think that's all.

Outright *topic avoidance* was attempted by very few learners, who, when they saw the object on the screen, said they had no name for it and made no further attempt to talk about it:

C2:   I don't know what's this. (laugh)

In comparing learners' and native speakers' use of communication strategies, we found that, on the whole—though not, as it turns out, in Tables 3.3 and 3.4—native speakers were more likely than non-native speakers to use the strategies of circumlocution and approximation—strategies which require certain basic or 'core' vocabulary (see Carter 1983), and sentence structures useful for describing, for example, shape, size, color, texture, function, analogy, hyponymy, and so on. ESL students who are developing strategic competence in English will need to develop such linguistic resources. In our research we have found that even advanced ESL students, who can use words like *economic*, *situation*, or *original*, may not be able to use terms such as *end*, *top side*, *bottom*, or *handle*—all useful expressions in describing entities. Certain linguistic expressions will prove to be useful again and again as similar exercises are repeated: for example, in the description of shape, *circular, flat, square, like a plate, bowl-shaped, triangular,* and also locative phrases such as *on each end, in the middle, on the rim, two inches from the top*; in the assembly of apparatus, instructional verbs such as *put, take, pick up, set down, turn.*

A nice subset of shape vocabulary to work with is exemplified by *bowl-shaped.* It is useful to make students aware of the way speakers within a culture may liken the shapes of objects to agreed-upon familiar objects, like (in English) bowls, cigars, mushrooms, and so on (cf. Nelson 1989).

In helping students acquire core vocabulary in a language, the teacher may profitably encourage the use of monolingual dictionaries, which typically use such 'defining terms' over and over again. Some dictionaries have lists of 'defining vocabulary' at the end—a valuable resource for our purposes.

To summarize, then, our research has shown that strategic competence involves the capacity to select effective means of transmitting information, and that a range of expressions are likely to provide that means. The particular expression used by an individual speaker is limited by the linguistic resources of that speaker, the speaker's knowledge of the world, and his or her assessment of the listener's knowledge of the language and of the world. Linguistic expressions observed as both native speakers and non-native speakers attempted to identify referents included both simple nominal expressions and more complex expressions, the more complex expressions seemingly being used when the speaker encountered problems in performing the referential act. However, the range of expressions used by native speakers and the range used by non-native speakers overlapped; some were used by both groups, some were more typical of the native speaker group and some of the non-native speaker group. Where communication strategies were used, the native speakers seemed to use more circumlocution and approximation than did the non-native speakers. Finally, there are clear differences between native speaker and non-native speaker groups in the level of detail provided in transmitting information; typically the non-native speaker group provided more detail than the native speakers seemed to feel necessary, though at times they also provided less.

3 Fostering strategic competence

Given what we know about the nature of strategic competence, what sorts of classroom activities are likely to promote the development of strategic competence? Here again, we shall argue that the same techniques which are useful for gathering data for needs analysis purposes will also be useful for classroom instruction.

It is only recently that language textbooks and program curricula have begun to include sociolinguistic and strategic competence as goals of instruction in the classroom. Although we now see an increasing number of textbooks and scholarly articles advocating a 'communicative approach' to the teaching of second and foreign languages, many such materials fail to clearly establish the nature of the 'communicative' skills being taught. Are the new materials designed to teach sociolinguistic skills, for example, linguistically appropriate speech acts, stylistic norms, politeness? Or are they designed to give the students guidance and practice in effectively 'getting meaning across', quite apart from grammatical correctness or situational appropriateness? Even when the goal of an activity is clearly defined, it is not always easy to evaluate whether that activity is effective in achieving that goal.

It would seem to be important for teachers and textbook writers alike to recognize that strategic competence is an ability which is distinct from both grammatical and sociolinguistic competence, and to be able to evaluate the effectiveness of classroom activities designed to foster it.

Classroom activities in this area may be designed either: (1) to promote the overall skill of the learner in successfully performing communicative acts, or (2) to promote the learner's ability to use communication strategies when problems are encountered. Most of the exercises in 'communicative syllabuses', such as exercises involving group problem-solving, are designed to give the learner practice in performing communicative acts in the second language, and thus to promote the overall strategic competence of the learner.

In our suggestions for teaching sociolinguistic skills, we argued for an essentially inductive, integrative approach with the prominent use of elicited native speaker data in identifiable contexts as a key element. We strongly encouraged an approach which put the learner in an interactive role with native speakers and used the classroom as a supportive situation where 'making sense' of the recorded interactions in retrospect could be undertaken. We took a very open view of how the learner might come to acquire a sensitivity to how native speakers express what they have in mind.

However, for the purpose of developing communication strategies, we feel that a more focussed and even explicitly didactic approach is possible. We differ in our approach from other researchers, who argue that communication strategies cannot be explicitly taught, and who would probably argue that we should use an inductive approach here as well as in teaching sociolinguistic skills. But it will become apparent that we feel that some of the needs analysis tools used in a task-based methodology may profitably be incorporated into language instruction which is explicitly focussed upon the development of strategic skills.

There are few, if any, materials available at present which teach learners how to use communication strategies when problems are encountered in the process of transmitting information. The language teacher can provide: (1) actual instruction in the use of such strategies, and (2) opportunities for practice in strategy use.

An instructional activity using a more structured inductive approach would be to ask student observers of communicative exchanges (where difficulties are encountered) to identify strategies which speakers seem to use when they do not appear to be able to find a precise name for an entity, and to evaluate the degree of success of various strategies. Such an activity amounts to asking students to develop their own taxonomies of communication strategies—an exercise which might help them develop an awareness of the frequency with which communication problems arise in the real world, and the variety of linguistic resources available to speakers for the resolution of such problems.

Classroom activities

One of the few classroom activities we are aware of which introduces the concept of communication strategies to learners was developed by Nelson (1989), and is reproduced in Appendix 8. Here, the students are given a definition of the term 'communication strategy', and a transcript of four (fabricated) conversations between a learner with limited English and an American. Students are asked to consider four communication problems which arise in the course of the conversation—one resulting from the learner's poor pronunciation, one from the learner's lack of familiarity with a term used by the American, one from the learner's inability to remember an English word, and one from the learner's inability to recall the past tense of *take*. Students are asked to evaluate the success of various strategies used by either the learner or by the native speaker to solve these problems.

Certain *initial* strategies may be more effective and economical than others (Nelson 1989). So, for example, in beginning to describe a crutch, it is probably better to begin by saying 'It's something you need when you break your leg,' than 'It's long and made of wood.' In another classroom exercise, learners are each given a set of cards with familiar objects depicted on them, and asked to tell another learner enough about the type of object pictured on each card for the listener to identify it. Nelson feels that such objects are best presented in *sets*: some objects are easier to identify when the speaker begins with expressions like 'It's a kind of' (for example, a photo of a racing car or a canoe); another set is best referred to with the expression 'It's a part of …' (for example, the steering wheel on a car); another group of objects seems easiest to identify in terms of function (for example, a corkscrew or a hammer), and a final set of objects seems easiest to identify when the speaker initially specifies the 'associated circumstances', or typical 'context of occurrence' of the object; so, for a billy club, 'A cop uses it', or, for a crutch, 'You need it when you break your leg'. Suggesting possible *best initial strategy*, or even sequences of strategy use, seems to be useful in the presentation of information on communication strategy use in the second language.

Another way of working with the same pictures is to use them in a 'vocabulary teaching' exercise (Nelson 1989). Here, the speaker may see a picture of a corkscrew, with the word 'corkscrew' labeling the picture. He then tells the rest of the class, 'My word is corkscrew. C—O—R ...' Then he tells what it is—using strategies, of course. The others write the word down, write a definition, possibly draw a picture. Most students enjoy the vocabulary work and having a written product which can be evaluated by the teacher.

In addition, students can be provided with core vocabulary useful for the strategies of circumlocution and approximation, either by instruction before undertaking the tasks, or by supportive instruction during the classroom exercise itself. We have already suggested the usefulness of the lists of 'defining vocabulary' found in some monolingual dictionaries.

One classroom approach might take advantage of evidence that individuals often perform speaking tasks like this better if they have previously played the role of listener (cf. Brown *et al.* 1984). It may be that the frustration of attempting to carry out some task on the basis of extremely poor spoken instructions motivates the listener to attempt to be more effective the next time he or she assumes the information-giving role. Thus, a few students might be asked to perform the task in pairs in front of the class, with the rest of the class, who have been provided with copies of the listener's task, observing. These classroom observers might be asked to arrive at their own assessment of the speaker's success in performing the task, and to list alternative linguistic expressions to the ones used by the speaker. Such a procedure would enable the students to learn from one another as well as from their own speaking performances.

Exercises providing the learner with practice in the use of communication strategies may focus upon any of several communicative acts. The exercises suggested thus far have primarily focussed upon the act of successfully identifying an intended referent (either concrete or abstract). However, learners may also be asked to give instructions to a listener on how to carry out a procedure, such as assembling an apparatus. For example, Brown and Yule (1983) asked native speakers to give specific listeners instructions on how to assemble a meat grinder; a range of assembly tasks of this type could easily be used in the language classroom. The speaker can be shown a series of pictures, or even a videotape, of the procedure, and then be asked to give instructions to a listener, who has the task of carrying out the procedure, or identifying the correct series of pictures. This task involves both description of the parts of the apparatus and mastery of a set of instructional verbs. (See Appendix 6 for photographs used in our research.)

Another variation on this activity would provide practice in narration: the speaker is shown a series of pictures or a videotape depicting several individuals in a story sequence. (See Appendix 7 for a series of pictures used in our study.) The listener who hears the speaker's narrative must select only those pictures which are described in the narrative and ignore others in the set presented. It should be mentioned here that in research using all three variations of this exercise (description, instruction, narration), the narration task seemed to be easiest for the learners to do—they were more fluent, and seemed more at ease and generally more familiar with this discourse mode.

Identifying the essential structure

In both the instructional (Appendix 6) and the narrative tasks (Appendix 7), an objective scoring procedure may be used to analyze the data in such a way that learners may be compared, not only with each other, but with native speakers of the language. As this procedure is described in detail in Brown and Yule (1983), we will here simply illustrate it briefly by using one of the tasks as an example. In this particular task learners and native speakers were asked to give an account of the procedure to be used in assembling a Christmas tree stand. As we have already observed, quite a bit of variability occurs in the various accounts provided on the tasks. However, an analysis of all the accounts reveals that there is an *essential structure* to each of them which may be identified. The essential structure of this task consists of those actions and objects which were mentioned by all (or almost all) the subjects in performing it. Once these actions and objects are established, it is then possible to compare the *ways* in which different subjects, or groups of subjects, realized them. The structure for the Christmas tree stand task was:

Put (three) object 2(s) through object 1.
Fit object 3 around (three) object 2(s).
Put (three) object 4(s) into object 3.

This essential structure based on the performance of both learners and native speakers now provides us with several points of comparison to use in our objective scoring procedure. For example, in performing this task, all the subjects mentioned object 2. It is possible to compare all the referential expressions used by both native speakers and learners to refer to object 2; these have already been provided above. Those terms used by native speakers may be employed as a norm against which to measure the performance of the learners. (In Yule and Tarone (forthcoming) we illustrate the procedure for establishing the essential structure of another of the instructional tasks used in our study.) Another way of using the notion of 'essential structure' is to establish the essential structure for a task based only on the performance of native speakers, and then to compare each individual learner's performance with that norm. For example, if *all* the native speakers mentioned the action of 'tightening' at the end of the Christmas tree stand task, this action would be part of the target essential structure of the task, and learners might be rated in terms of whether they included or omitted mention of this action.

All these are, of course, both speaking and listening activities. They can be structured so as to place the burden primarily on the speaker (by requiring that listeners maintain silence and do not ask clarification questions). But in real life, a complex negotiation occurs between speaker and listener, who work together to clarify the intended message. The teacher can provide instruction for the listener in these activities as well as for the speaker. Such instruction might involve the isolation, naming, and discussion of interpretive strategies such as appeals for repetition (for example, *What?*, or *I don't think I know that word*); mime (for example, puzzled facial expressions); questioning repeats (for example, Speaker A: *The water table.* Speaker B: *The water ...?*), and paraphrase (Speaker A: *The jugworm.* Speaker B: *The junkworm?*) An interpretive strategy often taught to counselors, and very useful for language learners, involves the use of frequent extended paraphrase of the speaker's message, as in *So you're saying that ....* Instruction in the use of such interpretive strategies may be very helpful.

Maintaining a balance

It should be emphasized that the exercises suggested in this section focus primarily upon the development of strategic competence in the second language. They will not necessarily improve either grammatical competence or sociolinguistic competence on the part of the learner. Work on strategic competence, both theoretical and applied, is in its infancy. What effect will classwork on strategic competence have on the development of accuracy in grammar and pronunciation? We do not know. It has been claimed, on the one hand, by theorists such as Krashen and Terrell (1983), that when learners are engaged in lots of interactions with native speakers in which they are focussed on meaning and not form, they will automatically get the right kind of input and will acquire grammatical accuracy. On the other hand, it is possible (as we have already pointed out in Part One) that once learners have developed communication strategies that enable them to say what they want, they may lose the motivation to produce more grammatically accurate forms. Higgs and Clifford (1982) argue for a balance between communicative and grammatical activities for precisely this reason.

That balance is, in fact, possible within the task-based methodology which we have described in this section. We have concentrated on the investigation of what learners do and do not know in terms of effective communication strategies. If, however, the learners' performance on the tasks is tape-recorded, then the teacher has an excellent resource for a future lesson on those learners' formal accuracy in using the language. While replaying parts of the tape-recording, the teacher can identify (or, even better, get the group to identify) aspects of the speaker's pronunciation or grammar which could be improved. For example, in a description task, one speaker said, *It is made by rubber—but it is cutted on front* ... With data like this, the teacher has ready-made material for a grammaticality-judgment and correction exercise for the whole group to take part in. The major advantage of using such data is that it works with examples of what *those particular learners* actually try to say. The learners' motivation to become involved in such an exercise stems from the simple fact that we are typically much more interested in what *we*, as individuals, say and do than in what some anonymous textbook characters might say and do. This type of activity is essentially a spoken-language equivalent of that process in the teaching of written composition whereby the teacher works with the learner and the learner's own production to arrive at a better version of what the learner tried to produce.

Another use of the tape-recorded data should provide the learners with an opportunity to compare the vocabulary used by native speakers in a particular task with the vocabulary they used. In one such exercise, an ESL teacher simply asked her students to list the verbs used by a number of speakers she had recorded performing the narrative task illustrated in 'The magazine story' (see Appendix 7). The pattern which emerged showed a distinct difference between the types of verbs used by two native English speakers and those used by two learners from different first language backgrounds. The non-native speakers used the following sequence of verbs: *entered/arrived—sat—saw—took—looked at/read —left*. The native speakers, describing the same events, used the following sequence: *walked in/came in—sat down—saw—picked (it) up—paged through (it)/looked through (it)—set (it) down/put (it) down—got up—left/went out*. With these different sets subsequently displayed on the blackboard, the teacher was able to elicit from her learners some comments on the fact that native speakers preferred to use phrasal verbs to describe the actions involved. What followed was an exercise on using a number of different phrasal verbs, according to the native speaker pattern, to recount another series of events depicted in a cartoon-strip story.

We hope that the language teacher will find the framework presented in this section, and the suggestions for classwork included here, helpful as models both in evaluating students' abilities in the realm of strategic competence, and in designing class materials which will enable learners

to be more effective in using the target language to perform communicative acts, both inside and outside of the classroom.

It will be clear, by this point, that the design of good tasks for both the
analysis of, and instruction in, the three areas of communicative ability
is of crucial importance. In the next chapter, we provide explicit
guidelines for the construction of such tasks, and examples of tasks
which we have used in our own work.

10   Some methodological issues in investigating learner language

In the previous chapters, we have examined issues related to the investigation of what the learner knows about the language. While we have been looking at different components of the learner's communicative competence, the procedures we have used to evaluate these different components have shared certain similarities. In this chapter, we focus upon methodological issues to be considered in constructing needs analysis instruments.

A number of identifiable factors must be considered in evaluating a learner's abilities in the second language. These factors break down, we believe, into those relating to the identity of the addressee, the topic of the discourse, and the procedures required by the task itself.

The addressee

In any situation involving communicative interaction, the second language learner will not simply be speaking in a vacuum—there will inevitably be someone to speak to. If an elicitation task intended to foster communicative use of the language is developed for the classroom, then it must provide an addressee who has some reason for listening to the speaker. Recognizing the importance of the addressee must also involve a recognition of the effect which the identity and role of the addressee can have on what the speaker says. In some circumstances, the grammatical forms used by the speaker may be strongly influenced by the particular addressee involved.

According to Speech Accommodation theorists like Bell (1984) and Giles (1980), the learner shifts styles in response to his perception of the addressee, either attempting to *converge*, making his productions more congruent with those of the person addressed, or to *diverge*, making productions congruent with those of some other group of speakers. Thus, for example, a learner speaking to a teacher of the target language might be *expected* to produce language forms which are more grammatically accurate than when speaking to another learner from his own country. On the other hand, some learners have been observed at times to produce forms with *less* grammatical accuracy when speaking to the teacher. A good example is Rampton's (1987) observation, mentioned earlier in Chapter 8, that ungrammatical constructions used by students seemed to be the students' way of stressing, for the teacher's benefit, their solidarity with their own culture and speech community over against that of the teacher.

We must not forget, of course, the type of convergence shown in native speakers' attempts to accommodate to the non-native speaker on certain occasions. The recorded interactions which we proposed in Chapter 8 sometimes provide interesting examples of native English speakers converging (by adopting specific expressions of the learner) with their non-native addressees. In the following extract, **M**, a Japanese ESL learner, has been talking about local Cajun cooking with **F**, a Louisiana housewife.

M: Yeah we went some restaurant and ate some Cajun food already—but ah—ah—people in Louisiana cook by yourself in my house—in your house?
F: yeah
M: cook Cajun food?
F: yeah—cook Cajun food—in my house

Speaker F's final expression will surely remind experienced language teachers of the ways in which their use of the language in the classroom is often influenced by the patterns of expression used by *their* addressees.

In light of these claims and observations with regard to the importance of the addressee in affecting variable speech behavior, when the language teacher designs tests to investigate the learner's ability to produce grammatically accurate forms in the second language, at least some thought must be given to the identity and social role of the addressee. To whom is the learner being asked to speak in this task? Can the learner be expected to converge or diverge in relation to the addressee, thereby producing language which is more or less grammatically accurate?

The elicitation materials included in Appendices 5 to 7 of this book specify that an addressee be provided for all speaking and writing tasks, outline a specific purpose for the communication, and recommend that the addressee *not* be the instructor (for a variety of reasons). Here we suggest that the identity of the addressee who *is* specified in these tasks should be considered when interpreting the level of grammatical accuracy used by the speaker or writer. While a detailed analysis of the relationship between addressee and grammatical accuracy would be extremely difficult to carry out under normal classroom conditions, teachers who are attempting to evaluate learner productions should nevertheless make an effort to:

1. be aware of the possibility of the influence of addressee on grammatical accuracy
2. allow for the possibility that their learners may not be aiming for grammatical accuracy in addressing certain individuals

3. begin watching for general trends in the way their students' language adapts to, for example, 'in-group' and 'out-group' addressees.

The topic

In normal communicative situations, learners do not just direct random language at some addressee; there is content and purpose to their communications, and there is considerable evidence to indicate that topic will affect grammatical accuracy in complex ways. Labov (1970) showed that, where the addressee remained the same, shifts of topic in a conversation, from, for example, evaluation of local politics to a description of a situation in which the speaker's life was in danger, correlated highly with style shifts. (Bell (1984) argues that the effect of topic is ultimately related to the addressee effect, in that topics which are normally dealt with in conversation with intimates produce the speech style normally used with intimates.) A topic-related factor which must be considered is the relative familiarity or complexity of the topic: Felix (1977) has convincingly shown that a learner who is forced to talk about an unfamiliar or complex topic in the second language may produce disjointed language and more inaccurate grammatical forms than when conversing about more familiar or simpler topics.

If classroom tests are to approximate normal communicative behavior, and yet also allow us to compare the performance of different speakers or writers, we must control topic. We cannot allow different learners to ramble on about general topics like 'Tell me what you did on your summer holiday', because then different individuals will end up talking about different topics: one will talk about his garden, another about her summer job, and yet another about a close brush with death while sky-diving. Learners need to be provided with tightly-controlled, narrow topics. Teachers need to decide whether, for example, they want a description of a concrete object or an abstract concept, instructions on how to assemble an apparatus or draw a picture, or a narrative of a particular series of events, and then provide the same stimulus material for all their students. Simple elicitation prompts which have provided effective topics for communication are photographs, pictures, and nonverbal video-tapes. These prompts can be held constant for all learners, so that comparisons across learners can ultimately be made. In the following pages we provide guidelines on the selection and use of such prompts and, in Appendices 5 to 7, give some examples of elicitation prompts together with instructions for their use.

In addition, the ability to hold topic constant in this way makes it possible to obtain *baseline data*—something which will be dealt with below as being all-too-often missing in our interpretation of results. And factors such as familiarity of the topic or complexity of the topic, may also be systematically varied in an attempt to determine whether, and how, these factors affect variable language forms.

The task

We have argued, in Chapter 9 and elsewhere, for a 'task-based' methodology to be used in the investigation of learners' communicative competence. Such a methodology, described in detail in Brown and Yule (1983) and elsewhere, provides a speaker with: (1) some pre-selected information to convey; (2) a listener who requires that information in order to complete a task, and (3) the awareness that an information gap exists. These three criteria are, we have argued, crucial for any elicitation task which is to provide the investigator with both spontaneous and, at the same time, controlled (that is, comparable) data.

In fact, we find a wide variety of tasks in use to gather data on learners' formal accuracy, and sociolinguistic and strategic skills in the second language classroom. Examples are tasks rating the grammaticality of target language sentences, correcting target language sentences with errors in them, reading minimal pairs and word lists (in the study of pronunciation), answering questionnaires, telling stories in response to tightly controlled visual stimuli, role plays, and responding to questions like 'Tell me what you did last summer?' In addition to the problem of maintaining topic constant, which we have just discussed, there are other task factors which vary greatly even in the brief list we have just provided, any of which may have an effect upon the formal accuracy, level of appropriateness, or communicative effectiveness of the learners' language.

The first point to consider is that these different tasks elicit different amounts of discourse—from single sentences to long monologues. On grammaticality judgment tasks, learners may not produce language at all, but rather read sentences and judge their correctness or conformity to some implied target-language norm. Some grammaticality judgment tasks may ask learners to rewrite or correct sentences which are incorrect, but often these rewritings may consist only of a word or two. Can accuracy scores on these tasks really be compared to accuracy scores on tasks where the subjects are asked to produce extended discourse in the second language? In addition to differences in sheer volume of data produced on these different tasks, the amount of connectedness of the discourse may vary considerably, from single, unconnected sentences to long, extended pieces of connected prose.

Second, the mode of discourse may vary, from descriptions and instructions to narration and persuasion. In the example cited above, the topic of 'summer holidays' could easily have led one learner to *describe* his garden, another to *complain* about her summer job, and yet another to *narrate* a close brush with death—thereby eliciting different discourse modes from different learners. And the language forms which we have selected to study may occur with different degrees of frequency in different types of discourse. For example, past tense forms are not likely to occur in the description of an apparatus. However, they are more likely to occur (but are certainly not obligatory) in narratives. Furthermore, as we have already seen, there is research evidence that different modes of discourse place different demands upon the language system, so that a learner may find it easier to be grammatically accurate within one discourse type than in another. Using carefully designed elicitation prompts will go a long way towards controlling discourse mode. The elicitation materials provided in Appendices 5 to 7 of this book are designed to elicit extended, connected discourse on predetermined topics, and to control the discourse mode produced by the learner.

Note that it is not enough for teachers to select a picture at random, show it to the students, and ask them to describe it. Such a procedure may not be much more effective at controlling topic and discourse mode than 'Tell me what you did during your summer holiday'. Rather, the following factors must be considered in choosing and presenting prompts in a communicative task designed along the lines of those in Appendices 5 to 7.

1   The prompts themselves must be carefully chosen to elicit a particular topic and not others. In observing an ESL class recently, we watched a student teacher run into difficulties because the picture prompt she had chosen contained a number of distracting elements. She had wanted a picture of a tennis shoe. But the prompt she chose showed a six-foot tall tennis shoe standing in a living room, surrounded by a number of astonished people. 'Just talk about the shoe,' the teacher said. But her students had a great deal of difficulty determining exactly what topic they were expected to comment upon simply because the prompt was poorly chosen.

2   The instructions given the learners will be crucial in narrowing the range of topics and the mode of discourse to be used with them. For example, if teachers would like the learners to give directions on how to assemble a piece of equipment shown in a series of pictures, they will have to word their instructions very carefully to ensure that their students do not simply *describe* each picture instead of providing directions for assembly.

3   Another aspect of the instructions should be kept in mind: a learner may be told to be careful to be grammatically accurate, or may be told that grammatical accuracy is unimportant. While the identity of the addressee and other factors such as setting may affect the learners' willingness to follow such instructions, we must assume that differing instructions may have different effects upon the language forms produced.

4 Another factor has to do with the amount of time allotted for the task. The accuracy with which learners produce certain language forms seems to vary systematically in relation to the amount of time they have to perform the task. Clearly, this factor of time must be related to the question of medium: writing typically allows one more time than speaking for modification of language form.

5 Ultimately, of course, teachers should try the prompts and instructions out on one or two native speakers before using them with their classes, in order to ensure that these do in fact effectively limit topic and control discourse mode in the way they would like.

Each of the three major features of the elicitation task: identity of addressee, topic, and task design, should be kept in mind in investigating grammatical accuracy, sociolinguistic appropriateness, and communicative effectiveness. The interested instructor, over a period of time, might vary some of these features to determine their effect upon the communicative behavior of particular groups of learners. For example, learners might be asked to perform the same tasks but with different addressees, and their language examined for variation under these different conditions. Or, the identity of the addressee and the other factors might be held constant, and only the operations required by the task changed.

The data analysis

In addition to deciding what sort of elicitation task to provide, one must decide how the data are to be analyzed.

The first point to be made here relates to the use of 'obligatory context' which has typically been used to analyze the occurrence of a target language form in 'natural' language data—that is, extended discourse over which the learner has had some control. Briefly, an 'obligatory context' for any language form is a linguistic context in which native speakers of the target language would be obliged to supply that language form in order to produce a grammatically correct utterance. An example might be:

Yesterday John hik___ up to Seven Lakes Basin.

Here, an 'obligatory context' for a past tense morpheme -*ed* is created. For any learner, the number of obligatory contexts for any target language form may be counted up, and the number of times the form was supplied in such obligatory contexts may be calculated.

There are many problems with the use of obligatory context in analyzing the occurrence of forms in natural discourse. It seems increasingly clear, for example, that many learners are quite adept at avoiding the production of some obligatory contexts for problematic target language forms. This will mean that one learner may have produced all the linguistic contexts of interest in large numbers, and another learner may not have produced any of one particular linguistic context. This will present massive problems for analysis, in comparing one learner with another. Another problem is that analysis by means of occurrence in obligatory context does not permit the analyst to identify cases of overgeneralization in the data—that is, cases where the target form was supplied in contexts *other* than the obligatory contexts. For example, the *-ed* marker might be observed to occur in all the obligatory contexts for the past tense marker—but the learner's hundred per cent accuracy in obligatory context may not mean that the form has been acquired; *-ed* may also occur *whenever* a verb is used by the learner, in contexts where no native speaker would use such a marker, as in '*You should walked.' Analysis in terms of the obligatory context would be unable to capture this pattern in the data. Alternative methods of analysis which allow one to identify cases of overgeneralization are needed and have been proposed by a variety of researchers (for example Parrish 1987; Pica 1984; Huebner 1983), and should be drawn upon when we analyze our data.

The second point to be made here has been alluded to earlier, and this is the importance of establishing good baseline data for the purposes of comparison. There are two components involved in establishing a baseline: first, the *essential structure* of the task must be established, and second, data must be obtained from native speakers. The establishment of the essential structure of the task (discussed in Chapter 9, and in Brown and Yule 1983) involves determining which persons and objects are mentioned by all, or almost all, the subjects in completing the task. Establishing the essential structure allows the teacher to then objectively evaluate the communicative effectiveness of individual students. In relation to the second component—native speaker data—far too often, classroom elicitation measures are given only to second language learners; teachers then go on to analyze the learners' performance and to suggest causes for this performance by comparing it with hypothesized productions of some 'ideal' native speaker of the target language. The point here is that real learner performance data are being compared to some idealized concept of native speakers' use of the target language, and *not* to real performance on the same tasks by speakers of the target language. Of course, for practical reasons classroom teachers must often rely on their own intuition in judging learner performance; it is not possible to norm *all* elicitation measures on native speakers. However, often a 'quick-and-dirty' check with even *one* native speaker can be very informative.

In a recent study (Gundel and Tarone 1984) which attempted to elicit production of direct object pronouns on several tasks, second language learners were asked to describe a series of pictures which were supposed to force production of direct object pronouns in referring over and over to the same entity. The learners, however, did not use direct object pronouns much; rather, they usually repeated the full noun phrase:

The boy sees a ball, and he picks up the ball, and throws the ball, and he sits on the ball, and he puts the ball in a mailbox.

Since the native language of these subjects did not require direct object pronouns, but rather allowed zero anaphora, initially it was thought that native language transfer might indirectly be causing some 'hyper-correct' behavior, since of course everyone *knows* that native speakers of English would not produce such a stilted piece of discourse. Fortunately, one native speaker of English was asked to perform the same task—and the same pattern occurred; probably something in the design of the task itself elicited the repetition of full noun phrases (or possibly we chose an odd native speaker!). In order to make valid interpretations of the patterns in our data, then, we need to ask native speakers of the target language to perform the same tasks which the learners perform, in order to establish a valid target baseline.

Finally, in analyzing the performance of second language learners on productive tasks, a very detailed examination of the data may be quite useful. For example, Lund (1985) who was studying learner accuracy on verb forms, listed the particular verbs used by individual learners in narrating the same story. He discovered that Learner A, who had a high formal accuracy rate overall, also seemed to have told the story using very few verbs, and all of these had simple conjugations, while Learner B, who had a lower overall formal accuracy rate on this task, had told the story using a wider variety of verbs, many of them requiring difficult conjugations. Our conclusions about the proficiency of these two learners, and the causes of their variability in formal accuracy on this task, may be tempered by such a detailed qualitative analysis.

We hope that the methodological issues which we have raised will be of help to classroom teachers interested in improving their investigation of their learners' communicative competence, as outside observers looking in upon the learner. In Part Four we attempt to explore the learner's abilities from the inside looking out—that is, the learner's perception of his or her own abilities.

Further reading

For a historical perspective on the origins of our grammatical tradition, consult the first three chapters of Robins (1979) or, for the pedagogical tradition, see Howatt (1984). The best available text on language testing measures is Oller (1979), while Davies (1978) presents a comprehensive review of the whole field. More recent guides for constructing tests are Cohen (1980), Henning (1987), and Madsen (1983). The original distinction between discrete-point and integrative measures was made in Carroll (1961).

Two very informative texts on the backgrounds of ESL learners are McKay and Wong (1988) and Swan and Smith (1987). A good text introducing and evaluating research on the development of inter-language is provided in Ellis (1985). For thorough accounts of the concept of interlanguage, see Selinker (1972); Tarone, Frauenfelder, and Selinker (1976); Adjémian (1976); Tarone (1979); Corder (1981), and the contributions in Davies, Criper, and Howatt (1984). A thorough review of grammaticality judgment research, and other similar measures, is presented in Chaudron (1983). Specific works using grammaticality judgments in second language acquisition which are worth consideration include Schachter, Tyson, and Diffley (1976); Bialystok (1979; 1982), and Singh, d'Anglejean, and Carroll (1982). A summary of research on variability in interlanguage is presented in Tarone (1988). Variability in the language addressed to learners has also been investigated in a number of studies, for example, Gass and Varonis (1985) and Long (1983).

For examples of research studies on second language learners' ability to perform speech acts, see Cohen and Olshtain (1981) and Olshtain (1983) on 'apologies'; Beebe, Takahashi, and Uliss-Weitz (forthcoming) on 'refusals'; Wolfson (1981) on 'compliments'; Eisenstein and Bodman (1986) on 'gratitude'. For discussions of the limitations of the questionnaire approach to the study of speech acts, see Manes and Wolfson (1981). Scotton and Bernsten (1988) provide a good argument for using 'real world' data in the study of speech acts. See Bodman and Lanzano (1983) for an example of an ESL textbook series based on second language speech-act research. For a discussion of Speech Accommodation Theory, see Giles and Powesland (1975) and Giles (1980). An interesting summary of research on the way social processes affect a learner's 'identity' and consequent interlanguage production is

Zuengler (1989). A discussion of script theory appears in Schank and Abelson (1977), and a description of the methodology used in researching scripts in Bower, Black, and Turner (1979). Collections of papers on sociolinguistics and second language acquisition appear in Wolfson and Judd (1983) and in Scarcella *et al.* (forthcoming), while the contributions in Rivers (1987) focus on interaction. Hatch and Hawkins (1987) present arguments for what they call 'the experiential approach'.

An extensive discussion of communication strategies, by a variety of authors, appears in Færch and Kasper (1983). Specific works dealing with strategic competence are Tarone (1984), Paribakht (1985), Yule and Tarone (forthcoming), and Bongaerts and Poulisse (1989). Discussion of the task-based approach can be found in Brown and Yule (1983) and Brown *et al.* (1984), Candlin and Murphy (1987), and in more specifically pedagogical texts such as Anderson and Lynch (1988) or Bygate (1987). Investigations of learner language in performing different tasks are presented, for example, in Doughty and Pica (1986), Long and Porter (1985), Porter (1986), and Yule and Gregory (1988). For an example of classroom-based research of a very useful type which focusses on the classroom use of a communication game, see Gardner (1987). Finally, for a discussion of practical classroom activities designed to encourage the growth of strategic competence, see Nelson (1989).

PART FOUR

Getting the learners' views

Introduction

Traditional language teaching, sometimes given the general label 'Grammar-Translation', seems in retrospect to have taken place in a much simpler world. The teacher, following the textbook, provided students with what they needed to know. The students' task was to learn the material. If, at the end of a course of instruction, the students could demonstrate that they knew the material, then they received good grades. Low grades were simply the result of truancy, laziness, or low intelligence. Although we are sure that many language teachers of the older school were sensitive to other factors which influence students' learning at the individual level, relatively little attention seems to have been paid, in any consistent way, to considerations of the whole process from the learner's point of view.

In recent years, this has changed considerably. Whether it is presented in terms of 'learner-centered education', or 'affective variables', or 'self-assessment', the importance of the learner's perspective is recognized in virtually all modern approaches to the language-learning process. The recognition of the fact that learners have needs in what may be termed the 'affective domain', which are at least as important as their needs in the 'knowledge domain', has resulted in the identification of a number of factors which are claimed to influence the learning process. Concepts such as attitude, motivation, self-confidence, and anxiety are frequently invoked in discussions of what makes a successful language learner. However, although it seems intuitively reasonable that such factors would have a general effect on any learning activity, claims about their specific impact in second language learning have been much more frequently stated than demonstrated. A simple reason for this is that these factors are relatively difficult to isolate and study by means of some objective research instrument. Anxiety, for example, may be a momentary experience for some individuals or a more permanent predisposition of other individuals, as Scovel (1978) has pointed out. Moreover, according to Kleinmann (1977), there is a difference between debilitating anxiety and facilitating anxiety which may be experienced by the same learner on different occasions. In simple terms, anxiety is probably not a single concept, varies in its effect within and across individuals, and must be viewed as highly subjective. Such properties not only make this phenomenon difficult to investigate, but tend to leave language teachers unsure about how to reliably identify anxiety, or indeed other affective phenomena, as the first step in possibly meeting their learners' needs in this domain. Such uncertainty probably means that teachers do very little, if anything, to investigate their students' affective state.

We have no easy answer to the problem of identifying the precise role of affective factors in the second language learning process. What we can do is consider some methods for discovering the learner's point of view and describe, in the following sections, a number of exercises which we have used to gain some insight into the way learners perceive their own ability and the effect that this perception seems to have on their learning.

Cohen and Hosenfeld (1981) discuss the methodology involved in research efforts to investigate the mental states of second language learners. They suggest that such efforts ask learners to provide data by means of two sorts of activities: (1) 'think-aloud' activities, in which learners verbalize their feelings, without attempting to analyze them, as they are in the process of, for example, writing or reading material in the second language, and, (2) 'self-observation', which involves more analysis, and is usually conducted *after* the learning has taken place. Self-observation may be elicited by means of questionnaires, diaries, and interviews.

Questionnaires

It would seem that the most obvious way to discover the learners' point of view is simply to ask them. One way to 'ask learners' is to use questionnaires. In the most famous set of studies on attitudes and motivation in second language learning, Gardner and Lambert (1972) employed a large number of different questionnaires with accompanying rating scales. Since one of the best-known distinctions to emerge from that work was the difference between integrative and instrumental motivation for language learning, let us consider the materials used to make that distinction among learner types.

American students were presented with a set of reasons for studying French and asked to indicate the extent to which each statement described their own reasons for studying French. The rating scale beside each statement had the following form:

Not my feeling at all ___: ___: ___: ___: ___: ___: ___ *Definitely my feeling*

Some of the statements rated in this way follow:

1. It will help me to understand better the French people and their way of life.
2. It will enable me to gain good friends more easily among French-speaking people.

3. It should enable me to begin to think and behave as the French do.
4. It will allow me to meet and converse with more and varied people.
5. I think it will someday be useful in getting a good job.
6. One needs a good knowledge of at least one foreign language to merit social recognition.
7. I feel that no one is really educated unless he is fluent in the French language.
8. I need it in order to finish high school.

Gardner and Lambert (1972:148) interpreted higher levels of endorsement of any of the first four reasons in this set as indicative of an integrative orientation with regard to learning French. The essence of an integrative orientation is that the learner views his or her learning goals in terms of being accepted as a member of the general French-speaking community. Identifying a learner with such an attitude, accompanied by other attitudes such as positive feelings toward France and French people, and a general interest in foreign languages, is essentially an identification of a well-motivated learner who will probably be a successful learner.

Higher levels of agreement with any of the last four reasons in the above list were interpreted as indicating an instrumental orientation. With such an orientation, the student approaches the learning of the second language with the more specifically utilitarian purpose of accomplishing some goal other than learning the language (for example, finishing school, or getting a job). The implication of such an attitude, along with others such as a general preference for America over France, would be that this learner would probably not turn out to be as successful in developing general language proficiency.

Variations on this general format have been used in many studies, and the results are typically correlated with proficiency scores as a way of discovering relationships between attitude or motivation and successful learning. However, we should note that there has been some criticism of this general methodology. Oller and Perkins (1978) and Oller (1981) present just two versions of a basic argument which states that, by using such questionnaire formats, the investigator has no real way of knowing what the learner was thinking when he or she completed the questionnaire. In a self-report format, the learners may select statements which, according to their own values, are self-flattering. Alternatively, they may select statements which they believe the questioner would like them to select, regardless of what their personal views are. If we do not know, on any occasion, what kind of values the learner is using in his or her choice of statements, we may in fact be measuring something other than attitude or motivation with regard to the second language. Moreover, as Savignon (1972) has noted, self-report indications of positive attitude seem to change in line with changes in achievement scores during a course of second language study. In other words, attitude becomes more positive toward a language when the learner experiences success in the study of that language. This point should lead us to beware of using measures of attitude as predictors of successful learning since the relationship of prediction may actually operate in the opposite direction: success in language learning may cause positive attitudes toward the language, rather than vice versa.

These problems with the validity of self-report questionnaires should also be kept in mind when they are used in self-assessment procedures. A typical example of a self-assessment form, taken from Oskarsson (1978), is presented here in English, though it would always be translated into the learner's first language.

Instruction: Imagine that you meet an English-speaking person from another country. He does not know anything about you or your country. Indicate your estimated command of the language by putting a cross in the appropriate box (*Yes* or *No*) for each statement.

	Yes	No
1. I can tell him when and where I was born.	☐	☐
2. I can spell my name in English.	☐	☐
3. I can describe my home to him.	☐	☐
4. I can tell what kinds of food and drink I like and don't like.	☐	☐
5. I can tell him about my interests.	☐	☐
6. I can tell him what I usually read. [etc.]	☐	☐

(Oskarsson 1978:45)

If we could consistently elicit valid responses from learners via questionnaires of this type, we would certainly be in a better position to identify specific learner needs in the second language. There are, however, rather obvious problems with the probable validity of the learner's responses. Even if the learner is honest and capable of accurate self-analysis, the choice of response will inevitably reflect each individual's interpretation of what the statements entail. One learner may interpret the statement 'I can describe my home to him' as involving a brief description of the external appearance of a house, while another may think that a full description of the internal layout with all the furniture is also required. If the first learner answers 'Yes' and the second learner answers 'No', then the teacher has no insight, via this format, into what these learners are capable of. Indeed, the teacher could be seriously misled about learners' abilities if responses on questionnaires of this type are taken at face value. We suspect that any information elicited via questionnaires really does require some independent verification.

Diaries, observations, and interviews

One form of self-report, the personal diary, has provided a number of interesting insights into individuals' perspectives on their language learning experiences. For Kathleen Bailey, later consideration of some of her diary entries during a French course made her realize how much anxiety she had been experiencing during the initial stages, as in this entry: 'I hope Marie will eventually like me and think that I am a good learner, even though I am probably the second lowest in the class right now' (Bailey 1983:74).

In addition to general anxiety concerning her French class, this learner was also inclined to view her ability in competitive terms, always in comparison with her perceptions of the other students. While many language teachers suspect that general anxiety and competitiveness may exist among their students, it is not often that the effects of these emotions can be ascertained. The advantage of a diary study is that, if the learner's introspection can be taken as reliable, certain phenomena such as missing classes or poor performance on a test may be recognized as having emotional causes. The disadvantages of using diary-type data in a classroom teaching situation are all practical. Many learners simply do not have the time to maintain a diary of this type; many might not be inclined to write honestly, knowing that the grade-wielding teacher would be reading it, and few teachers have the time to review the learners' entries and offer individual support when the learner seems to be experiencing general anxiety. Nor can we assume that every learner is capable of effective introspection in terms of self-analysis. Also, since the keeping of a diary would probably be done in the first language, it would seem that time and creative energy would be devoted to use of the learner's first language during a period when that time and energy might more beneficially be devoted to using the second language.

An alternative means of getting the learner's view is the use of the process of observation and interview. In our experience, this process has become fairly common in programs which seek to meet the needs of foreign teaching assistants in US colleges and universities. The interview session is also widely employed in writing programs to provide individual feedback to learners on their written work, following a practice developed in freshman composition programs. In the ESL classroom, the most typical format would involve the teacher observing the student making an oral presentation in the second language, and later discussing aspects of the presentation with the student. When the presentation can be videotaped, the teacher can help individual students to assess their own effectiveness, to explain what they were feeling or thinking at different points, and generally to develop a sense of how their use of the language is perceived from the listener's perspective. In a sense, this situation presents the ideal context for both getting the learner's view and also for identifying specific learner needs. It allows the teacher to explore, by means of the interview, what each learner intended to communicate, and to illustrate, by use of the observed data on the videotape, where they were successful and where they were not. While the luxury of individual instruction supported by videotape is rarely achieved in most second language teaching situations, the general point here is that the teacher can benefit from attempts to help individual learners to gain insights into their own learning process, particularly when a language sample produced by the learner is considered by teacher and learner together. Such a language sample does not have to be a videotape—it may be an audiotape, a student composition, or even a grammar exercise. The value of student–teacher conferences lies precisely in that they permit teacher and learner access to individual learners' views of the learning process.

In larger classes, it may be difficult to set up individual conferences. In such cases, if the typical language teacher is to get the learner's perspective, he or she must devise ways of doing so during class time with large groups. In the following chapters, we shall illustrate one investigative procedure which explores the effects of the learner's self-confidence on his or her second language ability, and which was designed to be 'doable' with groups of learners during class time.

11   The confidence factor

Although it is not always included in discussions of the language learning process, self-confidence is normally assumed to have an influence in successful learning. When affective factors are explicitly discussed, there seems to be a consensus that the general notion of self-esteem may be a crucial factor in the learner's ability to overcome occasional setbacks or minor mistakes in the process of learning a second language. According to Beebe (1983), the 'healthy self-esteem' of most good learners keeps them from thinking that their errors make them look foolish. Brown (1977) suggests that 'a person with high self-esteem is able to reach out beyond himself more freely, to be less inhibited, and because of his ego strength, to make the necessary mistakes involved in language learning with less threat to his ego' (1977:352). In Krashen's theory (1981), self-confidence is specifically identified as an important aspect of the 'affective filter' in that it enables the learner to encourage intake, or useful input. Conversely, we would expect that lack of self-confidence would be an inhibiting factor for learners and this receives some support from the report by Naiman *et al.* (1978) that teachers, in their survey, felt that poor learners lacked self-confidence.

There is, however, a practical problem in turning these general observations into specific procedures which a teacher can use to investigate this aspect of learners' needs. Teachers may form general impressions about which learners do and do not seem to have self-confidence as a general personality trait, yet remain unclear as to how those learners are coping with specific aspects of the language being learned. After all, there may be occasions when a learner's over-confidence interferes with the specific learning task at hand, just as a serious lack of confidence may prevent some learners from fully exploiting what they know. The absence of specific investigative procedures in this area may be tied to a general, yet rarely justified, assumption that a student's accuracy in performance (for example, answering a test item correctly) reflects confidence in his or her knowledge, and inaccuracy reflects lack of such confidence. However, we might ask if there is any relationship between the accuracy or inaccuracy of the answers a student chooses on a test and how confident the student is of the accuracy of those answers. We would be rather disconcerted if it turned out to be the case that some learners were choosing correct answers with no confidence whatsoever and choosing wrong answers with a great deal of confidence.

By stating the 'confidence issue' in this more narrowly focussed way, we may be able to identify specific points in the learners' use of the language where confidence plays a crucial role. The emphasis here, as at many other points in this book, is on turning a very general question concerning an aspect of the identification of language learners' needs into a more specific question which can be answered in a practical way. In this instance, we are interested in investigating the practical repercussions of learners' perceptions of their ability in the second language. That is, rather than investigate the effect of learners' confidence in their general ability in the language, we will look at the effect of the confidence learners may have in their knowledge of specific aspects of the language. Hence the questions to be answered: when learners choose correct answers on a test, are they highly confident of their accuracy, and when they choose incorrect answers, do they lack confidence in their accuracy?

To answer those questions, we need a format in which students would not only answer test items, but also indicate, as a self-rating exercise, how sure they are of their answers. Fortunately, there are some precedents for this type of investigation. In a study conducted by Kleinmann (1977), students were provided with a five-point scale (ranging from 'completely sure' to 'completely unsure') on which they were asked to rate how confident they were about each of their answers on a test. A very similar confidence rating format has also been used in the assessment of speech perception skills of hearing-impaired listeners (native American English speakers). Noting that a percentage correct score on tests of word recognition rarely correlated very well with listeners' own reports of their communication difficulties, Yanz (1984) demonstrated how confidence ratings could provide greater insight into aspects of the speech perception process by quantifying the way in which listeners cope with uncertainty in their understanding of spoken communication. This difficulty encountered by hearing-impaired listeners in understanding spoken messages is rather similar, in functional terms, to that experienced by second language learners. If listeners identify a message correctly, but have little confidence in the accuracy of that identification, they may hesitate or refuse to respond to the message until it is repeated or clarified. Examples of conversations with such second language learners abound:

NS: Do you wear them every day?
Ricardo: Huh?
NS: Do you put them on every day?
Ricardo: Wear?
NS: Yeah, do you (+ gesture) put them on every day?

Ricardo: Ah! No. Muy XXX.
(Hatch 1978:415)

Alternatively, a listener may understand a message incorrectly but, due to a high level of confidence in his or her ability, may fail to recognize that the perception is incorrect and produce a totally inappropriate response, as in the following exchanges:

WHO ELSE DO YOU PLAY CHESS WITH?   He play me.
HOW LONG TO GO HOME?   In bus.
WHEN DO YOU WATCH CARTOONS?   Aquaman.
WHAT DO YOU DO WITH LOBSTERS?   In morning.
HOW BIG WAS THE BOAT?   In Disneyland.
(Hatch 1978:421)

In both these cases, the learners are likely to experience communication difficulties. A means of identifying such learners when they are performing classroom exercises or quizzes is illustrated in the following sections.

Very confident wrong answering

In one study (Yule, Yanz, and Tsuda 1985), a group of adult Japanese ESL learners were asked to take part in a classroom exercise. They had to answer fifty questions, divided into four sections. (The complete exercise is included in the first part of Appendix 9 for use by teachers with their own students.) Each time a student had to choose an answer for a question, they also had to indicate how confident they were of that answer being correct by circling a number on a five-point scale, ranging from 'Completely sure' (= 5) to 'Not sure at all' (= 1). Some examples from each section may make the format clearer.

The first part was a twenty-five-item listening exercise. For each item in this section, the students listened to a tape-recorded sentence, while looking at that sentence written down, minus one word, as in this example:

When did they ____ him?   *fire/hire*   5   4   3   2   1

The students had to circle the word which was in the sentence spoken on the tape. Then they had to indicate how sure they were of their answer by circling one number on the scale.

The second section contained five items in which fairly idiomatic English expressions were included in short dialogs on the tape. Here is an example of one dialog (from the tape), followed by the set of answers presented on the answer sheet from which the student had to choose the most appropriate, and also circle one confidence-rating number.

Speaker A: Hey, John, did you pass the test?
Speaker B: You must be joking.
(a) John is sure he passed.
(b) John is not sure if he passed or not.   5   4   3   2   1
(c) John is sure he did not pass.

The third and fourth sections, covering grammar and vocabulary respectively, did not involve taped material. A set of ten fairly typical grammar test items were included in the third section. Here is one example:

She gave me ____ good advice.   a
                                    some   5   4   3   2   1
                                    a few

The fourth section contained ten fairly typical vocabulary test items, such as the following:

                                    exercised
I have ____ the piano for one year.   trained   5   4   3   2   1
                                    practiced

When we looked at the results of this exercise, the first thing we noted was that there was no polarization of the confidence ratings in such a way that all correct answers were rated 5 and all incorrect answers rated 1. There was a general pattern which showed that the average rating on correct answers was higher at 3.89 (out of 5) than the average on wrong answers, which was 3.29 (out of 5). Overall, this group of learners were more sure of their correct answers than their wrong answers.

An indication of the learners' perception of their knowledge, when they get it right, can be seen in a high average confidence rating such as 4.60 on one item (distinguishing between *pin* and *bin*), which all learners answered correctly. A quite different effect can be seen when a question appears to have been problematic. Despite the fact that seventeen of the twenty learners answered correctly on another item (distinguishing between *cloud* and *crowd*), their average confidence rating was only 3.35. This is a fairly extreme example of a general phenomenon whereby unexpectedly low confidence ratings can accompany correct answers. We suspect that this reflects some feeling among the students that their knowledge may not be accurate. This phenomenon may be characterized as *non-confident correct answering*.

Perhaps more intriguing are the results which indicate the opposite tendency. On nine items in the exercise, the average confidence rating for wrong answers was equal to or higher than the average confidence rating for correct answers. The most extreme example of this pattern involved one item (distinguishing between *hat* and *hut*) which thirteen students answered correctly, with an average confidence rating of 3.46, and which seven students answered incorrectly, with an average confidence rating of 4.29. In such cases, it is clear that the students' perception of their knowledge is very misleading. While this provides further evidence of non-confident correct answering, it also illustrates what may be described as *very confident wrong answering*. On another item (distinguishing between *John* and *Joan*), the twelve students who chose the wrong answer had an average confidence rating of 4.25 (compared to the 3.50 average of the eight students who got it right). This type of finding should prove particularly disturbing because it suggests that these students are, on occasion, tending to indicate that they are very sure they are correct in their identifications when, in fact, they are wrong.

It is clear that any assumption of a straightforward relationship between accuracy and confidence in answering test questions of this type may not be justified. When learners choose a wrong answer on a test, we normally assume that they need to review the linguistic feature involved in that test item. However, if the learners have chosen that wrong answer with complete (false) confidence, then they may be unwilling or not ready to accept that they are having trouble with the particular linguistic feature. If the teacher has some way of accessing those learners' perceptions of their knowledge on that particular aspect of the second language, then he or she may be in a better position to discover what caused the 'false' confidence and consequently deal with the learners' needs more effectively. On the other hand, if we discover that there is low confidence on correct answers, perhaps as a result of guessing, then the learners may have to review that aspect of the second language again. With this in mind, perhaps we should encourage learners to express their doubts, after a test is returned, on those items they were unsure about, even when they recorded correct answers. Most of the time, we only review wrong answers.

Individual self-monitoring ability

The preceding discussion has been based on a consideration of the performance of the group of learners as a whole. However, we also have some information on the performances of individual learners. If we believe that some individual learners may perceive their ability to perform exercises in the second language with some kind of 'false' confidence, then it would be helpful to have a way of identifying such individuals. Let us illustrate one technique for characterizing each individual's performance on the exercise. Table 4.1 (overleaf) summarizes the scores of one learner.

In Table 4.1, Learner A's choices of correct or incorrect answers are listed according to the confidence rating selected for each answer. So, the number of times the learner chose a rating of 5 is divided between his correct answers (23) and his wrong answers (0). The number of times he

	Ratings						Average confidence	
	5	**4**	**3**	**2**	**1**	**Total**		
Correct answers	23	5	6	2	3	39	4.10	
Incorrect answers	0	2	4	5	0	11	2.73	(Index = 1.37)

Table 4.1   Learner A's accuracy and confidence scores

chose a rating of 4 is similarly divided into correct (5) and incorrect (2), and so on for the other ratings. The total number of correct answers is 39, and of incorrect answers is 11. With the results set out in this way, we can calculate this learner's average rating on correct answers and his average rating on wrong answers. We do this, for correct answers, by adding $(23 \times 5) + (5 \times 4) + (6 \times 3) + (2 \times 2) + (3 \times 1)$, and dividing the resulting sum by the total correct (39) to give an average confidence rating of 4.10. For the wrong answers, we add $(0 \times 5) + (2 \times 4) + (4 \times 3) + (5 \times 2) + (0 \times 1)$, and divide the sum by the total incorrect (11) to yield an average confidence rating of 2.73. Subtracting the average confidence rating on incorrect answers from the average on correct answers provides an indication of the learner's tendency to choose high on the scale when he's sure he's made a correct identification (and it is correct) and to choose low when he's not sure. This tendency, represented in Table 4.1 by the Index figure (1.37), is a reflection of the individual's ability to self monitor when considering answers to questions. The higher the Index, the more likely it is that the learner can recognize when he is really making an accurate identification. Let us consider the performance of another learner to illustrate how a very low Index figure comes about.

	Ratings						Average confidence	
	5	**4**	**3**	**2**	**1**	**Total**		
Correct answers	22	4	1	2	2	31	4.35	
Incorrect answers	12	5	0	1	1	19	4.37	(Index = −0.02)

Table 4.2   Learner B's accuracy and confidence scores

Using the same calculations as in Table 4.1, we find a much lower Index (−0.02) for Learner B. This low figure is primarily caused by the learner's treatment of wrong answers. Basically, when choosing answers which are wrong, this learner tends to select relatively high confidence ratings. The Index here provides some evidence that this learner can be a very confident wrong answerer. Indeed, the minus score in the Index demonstrates that, on average, this learner is more confident about the accuracy of wrong choices than of correct choices. We would have to suspect that his inaccurate perception of his ability may have a detrimental effect on his progress in learning the language.

Accuracy and self-monitoring

The different Index scores in Tables 4.1 and 4.2 are not simply the result of one individual having a higher accuracy score than the other. In Table 4.3, we show how similar accuracy levels (i.e. number of correct answers) can disguise differences in self-monitoring ability (i.e. the Index of confidence rating).

Learner	Accuracy (out of 50)	Self-monitoring index
J1	41	1.68
J2	41	.39
J3	44	1.35
J4	44	.23

Table 4.3   Individual differences in self-monitoring ability

Despite identical accuracy scores, J1 and J2 have really different profiles in terms of their self-monitoring abilities. The same distinction is to be found between J3 and J4. Generally speaking, we would have to say that the accuracy scores of J1 and J3 are probably a more genuine reflection of actual ability (in coping with this exercise) than the accuracy scores of J2 and J4. The relatively high self-monitoring scores of J1 and J3 would allow their teacher to feel fairly secure that these students' performances on the exercise do not disguise any lack of assuredness concerning the material presented. These students do not appear to be confused about what they do and do not know. However, there are definite indications that students J2 and J4 could be feeling less assured. Their low self-monitoring scores are a useful clue to the teacher that these individual learners will need some further support in coping with the material presented, despite their relatively good accuracy scores.

This type of finding actually raises a number of other questions. We wondered if it was possible that the relationship between accuracy and self-monitoring ability would change over time during a course of second language instruction. We were also intrigued by the idea that we might have discovered a reliable self-assessment technique which would allow language teachers to investigate their learners' perceptions of their progress in acquiring certain second language skills. Our further investigations in this area are reported in the following chapter and placed within a consideration of a large-scale shift in perspective in the language teaching field in recent years.

12   The perception of improvement

The investigation described in the preceding section involves a study of learners' errors and their perceptions of those errors. Taking the discussion of learners' errors generally as a background to our own research, we have noted that there has been a fundamental change of perspective in recent years with regard to the treatment of errors in the language learning process.

For a long time, it was a tenet of language teaching that, if a learner's production in the second language was allowed to contain errors or mistakes, then there would be some negative effect on the learner's progress. This view could be expressed in quite moralistic terms: 'like sin, error is to be avoided and its influence overcome' (Brooks 1964:58). Consequently, teaching techniques were often structured in such a way that the teacher could control the student's production and minimize the potential for error. If any error did happen to occur, it had to be corrected immediately. More recently, there has emerged not only a greater tolerance of learner errors but also, to some extent, a relatively positive view of the occurrence of certain types of errors as evidence of progress. Arguments on behalf of this view usually point to an ESL learner's production of *foots or *womans as examples of an overgeneralization of the rule for forming English plural nouns which also occurs in the English-speaking child's normal process of acquisition. Arguments in support of this view focus on the creative aspect of both first and second language acquisition and use (cf. Dulay and Burt 1974). Errors can then be taken as positive indications of the acquisition process at work. They may be considered provisional forms which, for a time, serve a communicative function in the learner's use of the language and will eventually be replaced by correct forms.

Counter-arguments have, of course, been presented, based on the evidence of fossilization of non-correct forms, to show that, without correction, some learners will not progress beyond a certain error-prone stage. Indeed, according to Higgs and Clifford (1982:67), students whose use of the second language contains consistent grammatical errors which are not corrected in the earlier stages of acquisition may become 'learning proof', that is, unable to learn the correct forms at all.

The language teacher, presented with these opposing views, is left with no clear-cut guidance on how to view learners' errors. 'Should errors be corrected or not?' the trainee teacher asks. When advice is offered on this issue, it usually comes in the form: 'It depends on a number of factors, such as (1) the type of error; (2) the situation in which it was made, and (3) the student who made it.' As far as (1) is concerned, the teacher may be able to decide if the error is simply a one-time careless mistake or one that is recurrent and in danger of becoming permanent. The usual procedure is to ignore the first 'careless' type and note that the second 'recurrent' type may need some attention in a future lesson or student conference. Obviously, the larger the class, the harder it is for the teacher to keep track of individuals in this way. Regarding (2), teachers usually know not to interrupt, with minor corrections of grammar points, a learner who is the middle of some extended description or story. The correction can wait until a later time, particularly if it can be brought into an exercise where class attention is focussed on linguistic form rather than on message content. In (3), we have a more complex issue. If it 'depends on the student', then the teacher has to have a way of deciding what the individual student needs, in this respect, at that particular point in the learning process.

Many experienced language teachers have developed good intuitions about the ways in which different types of learners go through the process. They often recognize when a learner is going through a difficult stage, trying to cope with a new way of doing things in the second language, and can offer sympathetic support during that transition. Teachers seem to be able to identify some errors, in both production and reception, and even a general decline in overall performance at certain points, as a necessary part of developing new skills in the language. This phenomenon has been well described by Robert de Beaugrande as an aspect of all learning:

> In real life, a significant accomplishment normally emerges from a painstaking series of approximations that are technically wrong or unsatisfactory, but point the way to something better. ... Similarly, entry into a new, unfamiliar domain of more complex skills is necessarily marked by an increase in errors over the previous stage of limited, but well-rehearsed skills.
> (de Beaugrande 1984:26)

However, from the learner's point of view, that transition may represent a particularly unattractive prospect. If learners feel that they are 'getting by', in some sense, with a 'limited, but well-rehearsed' set of forms in the second language, then they may be unwilling to give up the security of that position to go through a period in which their performance in the language might seem to deteriorate. In modern psychology, a similar phenomenon is described as a form of 'proactive interference', in which the prior learning of one way of accomplishing some task actually interferes negatively with the new learning of an alternative procedure. This is not a recent discovery. More than a hundred years ago, the neogrammarians Hermann Osthoff and Karl Brugman described such a situation very well:

> When serious attempts at upset are directed against a procedure that one is used to and with which one feels comfortable, one is always more readily stimulated to ward off the disturbance than to undertake a thorough revision and possible alteration of the accustomed procedure.
>
> (Osthoff and Brugman 1878 (1967):204)

So, we have to bear in mind two interconnected aspects of the language learning process. There are transition stages involving the acquisition of new skills during which learners' errors may increase, and some unwillingness to go through such stages may result in learners failing to make necessary progress in acquiring those new skills. Simply recognizing the existence of these aspects of the learning process is the first step in developing an awareness of learners' needs in this area. Such recognition may enable teachers to make sense of some situations in which their students seem to make no progress at all or even seem to regress in their ability to cope with learning the language. The problem with investigating students' performance in such situations is that we are not really dealing with only their knowledge of the language or ability to use the language, but also with their perceptions of that knowledge or ability. The traditional measures of progress, such as tests, may only inform us that some students are scoring higher than they did on the last test a few weeks ago, some are scoring the same, and some are scoring lower. They provide no insight into what other factors may be contributing to the differential performance of individuals.

We encountered one such situation when the teachers of an ESL pronunciation and listening course found that their students' performance on tests often followed an erratic pattern. What worried them most, of course, was the fact that some students seemed to get worse, in terms of test scores, after weeks of instruction. That worry, experienced by most language teachers at some point, stemmed from the possibility, in their minds, that their methods and materials were not effectively meeting the students' needs. However, it was clear that many students, working with the same teachers and materials, were improving their test scores during the same period. If the instructional approach was really the problem, why weren't all the students 'suffering' equally? Since the instructional approach was one in which a lot of attention was focussed on the formal aspects of American English pronunciation, following Prator and Robinett (1985), with an emphasis on articulatory phonetics, we suspected that, for many learners, the experience probably qualified as 'entry into a new, unfamiliar domain of more complex skills'. That is, some of these learners had probably been experiencing some success in communicating with English speakers, outside the classroom, despite the fact that their English pronunciation, as measured by in-class exercises, was seriously flawed. (That their English pronunciation was in need of improvement had been identified by means of the oral interview test which led to their being placed in the pronunciation course in the first place.) Suddenly, these students' limited pronunciation skills had come under close scrutiny and they were being asked to abandon some of them and learn another set of articulatory skills. One would, in such a situation, anticipate varying reactions to the learning task. We set out to discover if there might be aspects of the students' performance, in addition to accuracy on test items, which could be measured and which might provide greater insight into how these students were coping with the learning task. Essentially, we wanted to know, in some way, how these learners perceived their own performance at different points during the course.

Since we had elicited information on students' self-monitoring skills by using the type of exercise described in Chapter 11, and illustrated in the first part of Appendix 9, we decided to use a modified version of this exercise as a phoneme identification task. Basically, we wished to discover if some students could be developing better self-monitoring skills during a period in which their accuracy on the test items was not improving. Alternatively, we might find that their perception of their abilities was suffering a decline during the period of instruction.

Measuring change over time

In this investigation, we worked with a fairly large group (sixty-seven students) of ESL learners from a wide range of first language backgrounds who were enrolled in sections of a pronunciation and listening course. The development of effective second language pronunciation skills seems to depend, in the view of many, on first developing particular listening skills. For Prator and Robinett, the first step in learning to pronounce in a second language is 'learning to hear and identify a sound or sound contrast when a native speaker produces it' (1985:xvi). This view is supported by others, for example in Paulston and Bruder's claim that 'self-monitoring is one of the most efficient techniques we have found for improving pronunciation' (1976:115). If learners have difficulty with their self-monitoring ability in the second language, then we might find that their ability to accurately identify relevant sound contrasts would not necessarily improve despite weeks of instruction. To focus our investigation on learners' self-monitoring skills in listening, we prepared and recorded a set of forty English sentences.

These sentences, included in the second part of Appendix 9 (listening exercise), were constructed in such a way that, in each sentence, one of the words could be replaced by another (which differed by a single phoneme) and still make perfect sense. Choice of contrasting English phonemes was made on the basis of information and examples provided by Nilsen and Nilsen (1971). For example, students would hear, from the cassette, *What did you say?* and be asked to identify which of the two words, *say* or *see* they had heard in the sentence. The student's answer sheet, also included in Appendix 9, thus contained forty minimal pairs and, as each sentence was spoken, the student had to circle the correct member of the pair. In addition, beside each pair on the answer sheet, there was a scale with the numbers 3—2—1, covering the range 'very sure' to 'not sure at all'. Students were instructed to indicate, each time they chose an answer, how sure they were of the correctness of their choice. The students completed this exercise (the first session) in the first half of the semester, and seven weeks later they were asked to repeat the exercise (the second session). The forty test items were exactly the same, but were randomly rearranged on the tape and then ordered correspondingly on the answer sheet for the second session.

When we considered the results of this investigation, we noted that the group's average accuracy score (number of questions answered correctly out of forty) had changed very little from the first session (27.51) to the second session (28.25). We did notice, however, that some subgroups of learners had improved their scores substantially while others had actually scored lower, after seven weeks of instruction. The direction of change seemed to depend on level of scoring at the first session. Generally, those who had scored twenty-four (out of forty) or less on the first session showed substantial improvement in accuracy during the second session. Those scoring between twenty-five and thirty on the first session typically scored lower on the second session. Among those scoring thirty-one and above there was variation, but an overall tendency existed toward higher scores. The amount and direction of change for each of these subgroups is summarized in Figure 4.1.

Considering this set of results, there would seem to be a greater possibility for low scorers and, to a lesser extent, high scorers (on the first session) to improve their performance (on the second session) while, for middle-level scorers, a deterioration in performance appears to be more likely. It may be that, as learners improve up to a certain level of performance on tasks of this type, they have to go through a period during which no gains, in terms of accuracy, are made for a while and even some loss of accuracy is experienced. Indeed, it may be learners going through this stage who cause language teachers to worry that their instruction is having no beneficial effect. After all, the expectation would be that, after seven weeks of instruction, performance on exactly the same test items would provide evidence of improvement. However, that expectation is based on an assumption that accuracy on test items is the most appropriate way to measure change in a student's performance. Let us look at an alternative measure, working with the same groups,

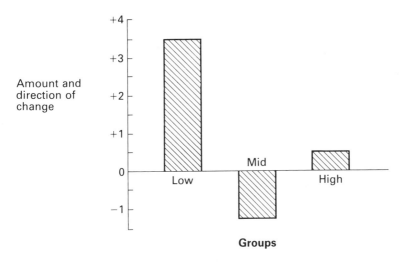

Figure 4.1 Changes in accuracy per group from first to second session

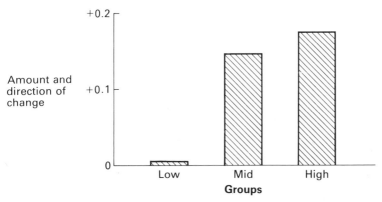

Figure 4.2 Changes in self-monitoring level per group from first to second session

which may provide a better clue to what happened to these learners as a result of the type of instruction received.

What improves when accuracy doesn't?

If we take the same groups of learners identified as low, mid, and high in Figure 4.1 and, instead of changes in accuracy, we use changes in self-monitoring ability as the basis of analysis, we arrive at the pattern of results illustrated in Figure 4.2. Self-monitoring levels were calculated for each session by arriving at the Index score (subtracting average confidence ratings on wrong answers from those on correct answers) for each individual. We could then calculate the amount and direction of change in self-monitoring ability for each of the three groups already identified.

The pattern which emerges in Figure 4.2 is rather different from that found in Figure 4.1. Note that, in Figure 4.2, there is no overall deterioration in self-monitoring level, and where we see little improvement, it is in the 'Low' group. For those in the 'Mid' group, who had shown lower accuracy levels on the second session, there is a substantial increase in self-monitoring level. There is a very interesting pattern to be noted here. It would seem that among low scorers (on the first session), there is no marked improvement or decline in self-monitoring level, despite the fact that this group showed the greatest improvement in accuracy level. However, for the 'Mid' group and 'High' group (on the first session), there are consistently better self-monitoring scores on the second session.

It may be the case that these three groups are, generally speaking, benefitting in different ways from the instruction they received. For the 'Low' group, the ability to choose correct answers on the test improved, but their self-monitoring ability did not. For the 'Mid' group, the ability to choose correct answers on the test actually deteriorated during a period in which their self-monitoring ability improved. For the 'High' group, both accuracy and self-monitoring ability improved.

Conclusion and speculations

It is possible that we have identified three broadly defined stages in the process of learning to cope with new skills in perceiving sounds in a second language in a formal setting. Those stages of learning might proceed something like this. In the early stages, learners may concentrate on simply making correct identifications of forms in the second language, perhaps even by guessing, and achieve some success. However, during this period, they are not very certain when they are getting it right and when they're not. During the next stage, particularly if it occurs in an instructional setting which encourages a formal analysis of the sounds of the second language, there is an improvement in the learners' certainty about when they are making correct identifications and when they are not, yet the number of correct identifications may decrease. This may be a period of great frustration for students, especially if they are giving up those guessing strategies they used to depend on and finding that their test scores do not improve. It may be that, during this stage, some learners simply choose to revert to the earlier strategies that yielded some success and elect not to continue through the process of developing better self-monitoring skills. That is, we may have identified some aspect of what is involved in the frequently-noted phenomenon of students reaching a kind of 'plateau' in their learning, from which they make no further progress. It should be pointed out, however, that there is a possible third stage during which learners seem to progress in both accuracy and self-monitoring skills with minor improvements still occurring.

Much of the preceding discussion is speculative. Yet it is speculation with a purpose. It is designed to create hypotheses which can be tested by further research. That research would require much tighter control on the identification of different initial groups of learners and a consistent tracking of those groups from the beginning to the end of a course of instruction (and, if possible, beyond). It might even be worth trying to reward the development of effective self-monitoring by informing students that their scores on the test will be calculated on the basis of the self-rating scale. That is, in the test instructions to accompany a format like the one presented in the listening exercise in Appendix 9, the following scoring guideline could be included for students:

Test scores
If you have the correct answer, you will *add* the number you choose on the scale to your score (i.e. *add* 3 or 2 or 1).
If you have the wrong answer, you will *lose* the number you choose on the scale from your score (i.e. *lose* 3 or 2 or 1).

It is our hypothesis that such a scoring system would not only allow students an opportunity for self-assessment, but would tend to identify low-, mid-, and high-level scorers more effectively. It would possibly allow the middle-level scorers to see any improvement in their self-monitoring skills being converted into higher test scores.

The greatest benefit of investigating these hypotheses would be the identification of students who seem, potentially anyway, to be at some 'plateau' stage. A system of rewarding gains in self-monitoring skills would offer such students greater encouragement and support to progress further instead of becoming frustrated and even slipping backwards. Making that identification would be a major step forward in assessing an aspect of the language learner's needs which we have tended to neglect for want of appropriate investigative procedures. We have suggested one such procedure and hope that other teachers will use it, improve on it, and benefit from it in future investigations of their learners' needs.

Further reading

Research on attitude and motivation in second language learning is summarized in Gardner and Lambert (1972), with more recent work reported in Gardner (1985), Stølen (1987), and Strong (1984). For less technical discussions of the influence of affective factors, try Brown (1973) or Chastain (1975). For views on how these factors, among others, help profile the 'good language learner', see Rubin (1975), Brown (1977), Naiman, Fröhlich, Stern, and Todesco (1978), and for Krashen's particular interpretation, see Krashen (1981, Chapter 2). For a general model of social and psychological distance which attempts to integrate notions like attitude, *anomie*, language shock, and culture shock, and a profile of a 'bad language learner', see Schumann (1978b). For a review of methodologies used to access learners' perceptions of their own language learning, see Cohen and Hosenfeld (1981), and for a summary of the validity problems of research involving affective measures and self-report data, see Oller (1981). A review of self-assessment approaches is presented in Oskarsson (1978). A review of a number of diary studies is presented in Bailey (1983) and a good account of one teaching couple's personal experiences as learners can be found in Schumann and Schumann (1977). On the risk-taking concept in learning a second language, see Beebe (1983). For more specific studies on the role of confidence and other affective factors, see Kleinmann (1977, 1978) and Murakami (1980) on learning English, and, on learning French, see Mueller and Miller (1970), Parsons (1983), and Samuels and Griffore (1979). An interesting study on the role of empathy in facilitating second language acquisition appears in Guiora *et al.* (1972). A rather technical analysis of the relationships among accuracy, confidence, and the self-monitoring skill, using quantitative measures from Signal Detection Theory, can be found in Yule, Yanz, and Tsuda (1985), with further investigations reported in Yule, Damico, and Hoffman (1987) and Yule, Hoffman, and Damico (1987). Lewkowicz and Moon (1985) provide a review of ways to involve learners in the evaluation process.

Bibliography

Adjémian, C. 1976. 'On the nature of interlanguage systems.' *Language Learning* 26:297–320.

Adjémian, C. 1981. 'La spécificité de l'interlangue et l'idéalisation des langues secondes' in J. Guéron and S. Sowley (eds.): *Grammaire Transformationelle: Théorie et Méthodologies*. Paris: Université de Paris VIII.

Alderson, C. (ed.) 1985. *Evaluation: Lancaster Practical Papers in English Language Education, Volume 6*. Oxford: Pergamon Press.

Allwright, R. 1986. 'Making sense of instruction: what's the problem?' *Papers in Applied Linguistics—Michigan* 1,2.

Anderson, A. and T. Lynch. 1988. *Listening*. Oxford: Oxford University Press.

Arthur, B. 1980. 'Gauging the boundaries of second language competence: a study of learner judgments.' *Language Learning* 30:177–94.

Bailey, K.M. 1983. 'Competitiveness and anxiety in adult second language learning: looking at and through the diary studies' in Seliger and Long (eds.) 1983.

Baker, C.L. 1978. *Introduction to Generative-Transformational Syntax*. New York: Prentice-Hall.

Bauman, R. and J. Sherzer. (eds.) 1974. *Explorations in the Ethnography of Speaking*. Cambridge: Cambridge University Press.

Beebe, L. 1980. 'Sociolinguistic variation and style shifting in second language acquisition.' *Language Learning* 30:433–47.

Beebe, L. 1982. 'The social psychological basis of style shifting.' Plenary address, Second Language Research Forum, Los Angeles, California.

Beebe, L. 1983. 'Risk-taking and the language learner' in Seliger and Long (eds.) 1983.

Beebe, L. and H. Giles. 1984. 'Speech accommodation theories: a discussion in terms of second language acquisition.' *International Journal of the Sociology of Language* 46:5–32.

Beebe, L., T. Takahashi, and R. Uliss-Weitz. (forthcoming) 'Pragmatic transfer in ESL refusals' in Scarcella, Andersen, and Krashen (eds.).

Bell, A. 1984. 'Language style as audience design.' *Language in Society* 13:145–204.

Bell, A. 1986. 'Respond to your audience.' Plenary address, 1986 Minnesota Linguistics Conference, Minneapolis, Minnesota.

Beretta, A. and A. Davies. 1985. 'Evaluation of the Bangalore Project.' *English Language Teaching Journal* 29:121–7.

Bialystok, E. 1979. 'Explicit and implicit judgments of L2 grammaticality.' *Language Learning* 29:81–103.

Bialystok, E. 1982. 'On the relationship between learning and using linguistic forms.' *Applied Linguistics* 3:181–206.

Blum-Kulka, S. and E. Olshtain. 1986. 'Too many words: length of utterance and pragmatic failure.' *Studies in Second Language Acquisition* 8:165–79.

Bodman, J. and M. Eisenstein. 1988. 'May God increase your bounty.' *Cross Currents*.

Bodman, J. and **M. Lanzano.** 1983. *Milk and Honey: An ESL Series for Adults.* New York: HBJ Center for Lifelong Education.

Bongaerts, T. and **N. Poulisse.** 1989. 'Communication strategies in L1 and L2: same or different?' *Applied Linguistics* 10.

Bowen, J.D., H. Madsen., and **A. Hilferty.** 1985. *TESOL Techniques and Procedures.* Rowley, Mass.: Newbury House.

Bower, G., J. Black, and **T. Turner.** 1979. 'Scripts in memory for text.' *Cognitive Psychology* 11:177–220.

Brooks, N. 1964. *Language and Language Learning.* (2nd edn.). New York: Harcourt, Brace and World.

Brown, G., A. Anderson, R. Shillcock, and **G. Yule.** 1984. *Teaching Talk: Strategies for Production and Assessment.* Cambridge: Cambridge University Press.

Brown, G. and **G. Yule.** 1983. *Teaching the Spoken Language.* Cambridge: Cambridge University Press.

Brown, H.D. 1973. 'Affective variables in second language acquisition.' *Language Learning* 23:231–44.

Brown, H.D. 1977. 'Cognitive and affective characteristics of good language learners.' Paper presented at the Los Angeles Second Language Acquisition Research Forum, UCLA, February 1977.

Brumfit, C. 1984. *Communicative Methodology in Language Teaching.* Cambridge: Cambridge University Press.

Buckingham, T. 1981. *Needs Assessment in ESL.* Washington, DC: Center for Applied Linguistics.

Burkhalter, A. 1986. 'The Expression of Opinions: a Preliminary Needs Analysis of Discussion Skills for Academic Purposes.' MA Qualifying Paper, ESL Program, University of Minnesota.

Butler, C. 1985. *Statistics in Linguistics.* Oxford: Basil Blackwell.

Bygate, M. 1987. *Speaking.* Oxford: Oxford University Press.

Canale, M. and **M. Swain.** 1980. 'Theoretical bases of communicative approaches to second language teaching and testing.' *Applied Linguistics* 1:1–47.

Candlin, C.N. and **D.F. Murphy.** (eds.) 1987. *Language Learning Tasks.* London: Prentice-Hall International.

Carroll, J. 1961. 'Fundamental considerations in testing for English proficiency of foreign students' in *Testing the English Proficiency of Foreign Students.* Washington, DC: Center for Applied Linguistics. Reprinted 1972 in H.B. Allen and R.N. Campbell (eds.): *Teaching English as a Second Language: A Book of Readings.* New York: McGraw-Hill.

Carter, R. 1982. 'A note on core vocabulary.' *Nottingham Linguistic Circular* 11:39–51.

Carter, R. 1987. 'Is there a core vocabulary?' *Applied Linguistics* 8:178–93.

Celce-Murcia, M. and **D. Larsen-Freeman.** 1983. *The Grammar Book.* Rowley, Mass.: Newbury House.

Celce-Murcia, M. and **L. McIntosh.** (eds.) 1979. *Teaching English as a Second or Foreign Language.* Rowley, Mass.: Newbury House.

Chastain, K. 1975. 'Affective and ability factors in second language acquisition.' *Language Learning* 25:153–61.

Chaudron, C. 1983. 'Research on metalinguistic judgments: a review of theory, methods and results.' *Language Learning* 33:343–78.

Chaudron, C. 1986. 'The interaction of quantitative and qualitative approaches to research: a view of the second language classroom.' *TESOL Quarterly* 20:709–18.

Chaudron, C. 1988. *Second Language Classrooms: Research on Teaching and Learning*. Cambridge: Cambridge University Press.

Chomsky, N. 1957. *Syntactic Structures*. The Hague: Mouton.

Chomsky, N. 1964. *Current Issues in Linguistic Theory*. The Hague: Mouton.

Chomsky, N. 1965. *Aspects of the Theory of Syntax*. Cambridge, Mass.: MIT Press.

Cohen, A. 1980. *Testing Language Ability in the Classroom*. Rowley, Mass.: Newbury House.,

Cohen, A. and C. Hosenfeld. 1981. 'Some uses of mentalistic data in second language research.' *Language Learning*. 31: 285–314.

Cohen, A. and E. Olshtain. 1981. 'Developing a measure of sociocultural competence: the case of apology.' *Language Learning* 31:113–34.

Cohen, A. and M. Robbins. 1976. 'Toward assessing interlanguage performance: the relationship between selected errors, learners' characteristics and learners' explanations.' *Language Learning* 26:45–66.

Connor, U. and R.B. Kaplan. (eds.) 1987. *Writing Across Languages: Analysis of Second Language Text*. Reading, Mass.: Addison-Wesley.

Cooray, M. 1967. 'The English passive voice.' *English Language Teaching* 21:203–10.

Corder, S.P. 1981. *Error Analysis and Interlanguage*. Oxford: Oxford University Press.

Cronbach, L.J. and P.E. Meehl. 1955. 'Construct validity in psychological tests.' *Psychological Bulletin* 52:281–302.

Davies, A. 1978. 'Language Testing, Parts I and II.' *Language Teaching and Linguistics Abstracts* 11:145–59; 215–31.

Davies, A., C. Criper. and A.P.R. Howatt. (eds.) 1984. *Interlanguage*. Edinburgh: Edinburgh University Press.

de Beaugrande, R. 1984. *Text Production*. Norwood, NJ: Ablex Publishing.

Dickerson, L. 1974. 'Internal and External Patterning of Phonological Variability in the Speech of Japanese Learners of English.' Ph.D. Dissertation, University of Illinois.

Dickerson, L. 1975. 'The learner's interlanguage as a system of variable rules.' *TESOL Quarterly* 9:401–7.

Dickerson, W. 1976. 'The psycholinguistic unity of language learning and language change.' *Language Learning* 26:215–31. Reprinted 1987 in G. Ioup and S. Weinberger (eds.): *Interlanguage Phonology*. Rowley, Mass.: Newbury House.

Dickerson, L. and W. Dickerson. 1977. 'Interlanguage phonology: current research and future directions' in S.P. Corder and E. Roulet (eds.): *The Notions of Simplification, Interlanguages and Pidgins: Actes du 5ème Colloque de Linguistique Appliquée de Neuchâtel*. Geneva: Droz et Université de Neuchâtel.

Di Pietro, R. 1987. *Strategic Interaction: Learning Languages Through Scenarios*. Cambridge: Cambridge University Press.

Doughty, C. and T. Pica. 1986. 'Information-gap tasks: do they facilitate second language acquisition?' *TESOL Quarterly* 20:305–25.

Dubin, F. and E. Olshtain. 1986. *Course Design: Developing Programs and Materials for Language Learning*. Cambridge: Cambridge University Press.

Dulay, H. and M. Burt. 1974. 'A new perspective on the creative construction process in child second language acquisition.' *Language Learning* 24:253–78.

Eisenstein, M. and J. Bodman. 1986. '"I very appreciate": expressions of gratitude by native and non-native speakers of American English.' *Applied Linguistics* 7:167–85.

Ellis, R. 1985. *Understanding Second Language Acquisition*. Oxford: Oxford University Press.

Færch, C. and G. Kasper. 1983. *Strategies in Interlanguage Communication*. New York: Longman.

Felix, S. 1977. 'How reliable are experimental data?' Paper presented at the Eleventh Annual TESOL Conference, Miami, Florida.

Freire, P. 1970. *Pedagogy of the Oppressed*. New York: Herder and Herder.

Gaies, S. 1983. 'Learner feedback: an exploratory study of its role in the second language classroom' in Seliger and Long (eds.) 1983.

Gardner, D. 1987. 'Communication games: do we know what we're talking about?' *ELT Journal* 41:19–24.

Gardner, R.C. 1985. *Social Psychology and Second Language Learning: The Role of Attitudes and Motivation*. London: Edward Arnold.

Gardner, R.C. and W.E. Lambert. 1972. *Attitudes and Motivation in Second Language Learning*. Rowley, Mass.: Newbury House.

Gass, S. and E.M. Varonis. 1985. 'Variation in native speaker speech modification to non-native speakers.' *Studies in Second Language Acquisition* 7:37–58.

George, H.V. 1963. 'A verb-form frequency count.' *English Language Teaching* 18:31–7.

Giles, H. 1980. 'Accommodation theory: some new directions' in S. de Silva (ed.): *Aspects of Linguistic Behavior*. York: York University Press.

Giles, H. and P. Powesland. 1975. *Speech Style and Social Evaluation*. London: Academic Press.

Givón, T. 1979. *On Understanding Grammar*. New York: Academic Press.

Gregg, K.R. 1984. 'Krashen's monitor and Occam's razor.' *Applied Linguistics* 5:79–100.

Gregg, K.R. 1986. 'Review of *The Input Hypothesis*.' *TESOL Quarterly* 20:116–22.

Grotjahn, R. 1988. 'Introducing (applied) linguists to statistics.' *Studies in Second Language Acquisition* 10: 63–8.

Guiora, A., B. Beit-Hallahani, R. Brannon, C. Dull, and T. Scovel. 1972. 'The effects of experimentally induced changes in ego states on pronunciation ability in a second language: an exploratory study.' *Comprehensive Psychiatry* 13:421–8.

Gundel, J. and E. Tarone. 1984. 'Language transfer and the acquisition of pronominal anaphora' in S. Gass and L. Selinker (eds.): *Language Transfer in Language Learning*. Rowley, Mass.: Newbury House.

Hanges, K. 1982. 'Course Design for a Composition/Research Skills Class for International Graduate Students.' MA Qualifying Paper, ESL Program, University of Minnesota.

Hatch, E. 1978. 'Discourse analysis and second-language acquisition' in E. Hatch (ed.): *Second Language Acquisition*. Rowley, Mass.: Newbury House.

Hatch, E. and H. Farhady. 1982. *Research Design and Statistics for Applied Linguistics*. Rowley, Mass.: Newbury House.

Hatch, E. and B. Hawkins. 1987. 'Second language acquisition: an experiential approach' in S. Rosenberg (ed.): *Advances in Applied Psycholinguistics*, Vol. 2. Cambridge: Cambridge University Press.

Heath, S.B. 1986. 'Children at risk? Building investments in diversity.' Plenary address, TESOL Annual Meeting, Anaheim, California.

Heaton, J.B. 1975. *Writing English Language Tests*. London: Longman.

Henning, G. 1986. 'Quantitative methods in language acquisition research.' *TESOL Quarterly* 20:701–8.

Henning, G. 1987. *A Guide to Language Testing*. Rowley, Mass.: Newbury House.

Higgs, T.V. and **R. Clifford.** 1982. 'The push toward communication' in T.V. Higgs (ed.): *Curriculum, Competence and the Foreign Language Teacher*. Skokie, Ill.: National Textbook Co.

Horowitz, D.M. 1986. 'What professors actually require: academic tasks for the ESL classroom.' *TESOL Quarterly* 20:445–62.

Howatt, A.P.R. 1984. *A History of English Language Teaching*. Oxford: Oxford University Press.

Huebner, T. 1983. *A Longitudinal Analysis of the Acquisition of English*. Ann Arbor, Mich.: Karoma Publishers.

Huebner, T. 1985. 'System and variability in syntax.' *Language Learning* 35:141–64.

Hutchinson, T. and **A. Waters.** 1980. 'ESP at the crossroads.' *English for Special Purposes Newsletter* III (36). Corvallis, Oregon: English Language Institute, Oregon State University.

Hutchinson, T. and **A. Waters.** 1987. *English for Specific Purposes*. Cambridge: Cambridge University Press.

Hymes, D. 1971. *On Communicative Competence*. Philadelphia, Pa.: University of Pennsylvania Press.

Jacobson, W. 1987. 'An assessment of the communication needs of non-native speakers of English in an undergraduate physics lab.' *ESP Journal* 5: 173–88.

Jenks, F. 1981. 'Learners' needs and the selection of compatible materials' in J.E. Alatis *et al.* (eds.): *The Second Language Classroom: Directions for the 1980's: Essays in Honor of Mary Finocchiaro*. New York: Oxford University Press.

Jespersen, O. 1933. *Essentials of English Grammar*. London: Allen and Unwin.

Johns, A. 1988. 'The discourse communities dilemma: identifying transferable skills for the academic milieu.' *English for Specific Purposes* 7:55–9.

Johnson, K. 1982. *Communicative Syllabus Design and Methodology*. Oxford: Pergamon Press.

Johnson, K. 1983. 'Syllabus design: possible future trends' in K. Johnson and D. Porter (eds.): *Perspectives in Communicative Language Teaching*. New York: Academic Press.

Jones, L. and **C. Von Baer.** 1983. *Functions of American English*. Cambridge: Cambridge University Press.

Kagan, S. 1985. *Cooperative Learning*. Laguna Niguel, Calif.: Resources for Teachers.

Klein, W. 1986. *Second Language Acquisition*. Cambridge: Cambridge University Press.

Kleinmann, H.H. 1977. 'Avoidance behavior in adult second language acquisition.' *Language Learning* 27:93–108.

Kleinmann, H.H. 1978. 'The strategy of avoidance in adult second language acquisition' in W.C. Ritchie (ed.): *Second Language Acquisition Research: Issues and Implications*. New York: Academic Press.

Krashen, S. 1981. *Second Language Acquisition and Second Language Learning*. Oxford: Pergamon Press.

Krashen, S. 1982. *Principles and Practice in Second Language Acquisition*. Oxford: Pergamon Press.

Krashen, S. 1985. *Inquiries and Insights*. Hayward, Calif.: Alemany Press.
Krashen, S. and Terrell, T. 1983. *The Natural Approach*. Hayward, Calif.: Alemany Press.

Labov, W. 1970. 'The study of language in its social context.' *Studium Generale* 23:30–87.
Labov, W. 1975. *What Is a Linguistic Fact?* Lisse, Belgium: Peter de Ridder Press.
Lackstrom, J., L. Selinker, and L. Trimble. 1972. 'Technical rhetorical principles and grammatical choice.' *TESOL Quarterly* 7:127–36.
Lado, R. 1961. *Language Testing*. New York: McGraw-Hill.
Larsen-Freeman, D. 1986. *Principles and Techniques in Language Teaching*. Oxford: Oxford University Press.
Levinson, S.C. 1983. *Pragmatics*. Cambridge: Cambridge University Press.
Lewkowicz, J. and J. Moon. 1985. 'Evaluation: a way of involving the learner' in C. Alderson (ed.) 1985.
Long, M. 1983. 'Linguistic and conversational adjustment to non-native speakers.' *Studies in Second Language Acquisition* 5:177–93.
Long, M. and P. Porter. 1985. 'Group work, interlanguage talk, and second language acquisition.' *TESOL Quarterly* 19:207–28.
Lund, R. 1985. 'The Formal Accuracy of College German Students with the Finite Verb on Communicative Production and Linguistic Awareness Tasks.' Ph.D. Dissertation, University of Minnesota.

Mackay, R. 1981. 'Developing a reading curriculum for ESP' in Selinker, Tarone, and Hanzeli (eds.) 1981.
Mackey, W. 1965. *Language Teaching Analysis*. Bloomington, Ind.: Indiana University Press.
Maclay, H. and M.D. Sleator. 1960. 'Responses to language: judgments of grammaticalness.' *International Journal of American Linguistics* 26:275–82.
Madsen, H.S. 1983. *Techniques in Testing*. Oxford: Oxford University Press.
Manes, J. and N. Wolfson. 1981. 'The compliment formula' in F. Coulmas (ed.): *Conversational Routine*. The Hague: Mouton.
McKay, S.L. and S.C. Wong. (eds.) 1988. *Language Diversity: Problem or Resource?* Rowley, Mass.: Newbury House.
McLaughlin, B. 1978. 'The Monitor Model: some methodological considerations.' *Language Learning* 28:309–32.
McLaughlin, B. 1987. *Theories of Second Language Learning*. London: Edward Arnold.
McLaughlin, M. 1984. *Conversation: How Talk is Organized*. Beverly Hills, Calif.: Sage Publications.
Medgyes, P. 1986. 'Queries from a communicative teacher.' *English Language Teaching Journal* 40:107–12.
Morrow, K. and K. Johnson. 1979. *Communicate*. Cambridge: Cambridge University Press.
Mueller, T.H. and R.I. Miller. 1970. 'A study of student attitudes and motivation in a collegiate French course using programmed learning instruction.' *IRAL* 8:297–320.
Munby, J. 1978. *Communicative Syllabus Design*. Cambridge: Cambridge University Press.
Murakami, M. 1980. 'Behavioral and attitudinal correlates of progress in ESL by native speakers of Japanese' in J.W. Oller and K. Perkins (eds.): *Research in Language Testing*. Rowley, Mass.: Newbury House.

Myers, G. 1989. 'The pragmatics of politeness in scientific articles.' *Applied Linguistics* 10: 1–35.

Naiman, N., M. Fröhlich, H.H. Stern, and **A. Todesco.** 1978. *The Good Language Learner*. Toronto: Ontario Institute for Studies in Education.
Nelson, E. 1989. 'Teaching communication strategies.' Unpublished manuscript, Minnesota English Center, University of Minnesota.
Newmeyer, F. 1983. *Grammatical Theory: Its Limits and Its Possibilities*. Chicago: University of Chicago Press.
Nilsen, D. and **A. Nilsen.** 1971. *Pronunciation Contrasts in English*. New York: Regents Publishing.

Oller, J. 1979. *Language Tests at School: A Pragmatic Approach*. London: Longman.
Oller, J. 1981. 'Can affect be measured?' *IRAL* 19:227–35.
Oller, J. and **K. Perkins.** 1978. 'Intelligence and language proficiency as sources of variance in self-reported affective variables.' *Language Learning* 28:85–97.
Oller, J. and **P. Richard-Amato.** 1983. *Methods that Work*. Rowley, Mass.: Newbury House.
Olshtain, E. 1983. 'Sociocultural competence and language transfer: the case of apology' in S. Gass and L. Selinker (eds.): *Language Transfer in Language Learning*. Rowley, Mass.: Newbury House.
Oskarsson, M. 1978. *Approaches to Self-Assessment in Foreign Langue Learning*. Oxford: Pergamon Press.
Oster, S. 1981. 'The use of tenses in "reporting past literature" in EST' in Selinker, Tarone, and Hanzeli (eds.) 1981.
Osthoff, H. and **K. Brugman.** 1878 (1967). 'Morphological investigations' in W.P. Lehman (ed.): *A Reader in Nineteenth Century Historical Indo-European Linguistics*. Bloomington, Ind.: Indiana University Press.

Paribakht, T. 1982. 'The Relationship Between the Use of Communication Strategies and Aspects of Target Language Proficiency: a Study of Persian ESL Students.' Ph.D. Dissertation, University of Toronto.
Paribakht, T. 1985. 'Strategic competence and language proficiency.' *Applied Linguistics* 6:132–46.
Parrish, B. 1987. 'A new look at methodologies in the study of article acquisition for learners of ESL.' *Language Learning* 37:361–84.
Parsons, A.H. 1983. 'Self-esteem and the acquisition of French' in K.M. Bailey, M.H. Long, and S. Peck (eds.): *Second Language Acquisition Studies: Series on Issues in Second Language Research*. Rowley, Mass.: Newbury House.
Patton, M.Q. 1981. *Alternative Evaluation Research Paradigm*. Beverly Hills, Calif.: Sage Publications.
Paulston, C.B. and **M. Bruder.** 1976. *Teaching English as a Second Language*. Cambridge, Mass.: Winthrop Press.
Pica, T. 1984. 'Procedures for morpheme data analysis in second language acquisition research.' Paper presented at the 1984 TESOL Convention, Houston, Texas.
Porter, P. 1986. 'How learners talk to each other: input and interaction in task-centered discussions' in R.R. Day (ed.): *Talking to Learn*. Rowley, Mass.: Newbury House.
Powell, W. and **C. Taylor,** 1985. 'The language-learning valise: the neglected piece

of cultural baggage.' Paper presented at the First Southeastern Regional TESOL Conference, Atlanta, Georgia.

Prabhu, N.S. 1987. *Second Language Pedagogy.* Oxford: Oxford University Press.

Prator, C. and **B.W. Robinett.** 1985. *Manual of American English Pronunciation.* New York: Holt, Rinehart and Winston.

Purves, A.C. and **W.C. Purves.** 1986. 'Viewpoints: cultures, text models and the activity of writing.' *Research in the Teaching of English* 20:174–97.

Rampton, B. 1987. 'Stylistic variability and not speaking "normal" English' in R. Ellis (ed.): *Second Language Acquisition in Context.* London: Prentice-Hall International.

Ranney, S. 1986. 'The Medical Consultation in the U.S. and Japan: an Investigation of a Speech Event with Elicited Scripts.' Unpublished paper, ESL Program, University of Minnesota.

Richard-Amato, P.A. 1988. *Making it Happen.* London: Longman.

Richards, J. 1984. 'The secret life of methods.' *TESOL Quarterly* 18:7–23.

Richards, J. and **T.S. Rodgers.** 1986. *Approaches and Methods in Language Teaching.* Cambridge: Cambridge University Press.

Richterich, R. 1983. *Case Studies in Identifying Language Needs.* Oxford: Pergamon Press.

Richterich, R. and **J.L. Chancerel.** 1980. *Identifying the Needs of Adults Learning a Foreign Language.* Oxford: Pergamon Press.

Rivera, C. (ed.) 1984. *Communicative Competence Approaches to Language Proficiency Assessment: Research and Application.* Clevedon, England: Multilingual Matters Ltd.

Rivers, W. 1983. *Speaking in Many Tongues.* Cambridge: Cambridge University Press.

Rivers, W. (ed.) 1987. *Interactive Language Teaching.* Cambridge: Cambridge University Press.

Robins, R.H. 1979. *A Short History of Linguistics.* London: Longman.

Rubin, J. 1975. 'What the "good language learner" can teach us.' *TESOL Quarterly* 9:41–51.

Rutherford, W. and **M. Sharwood-Smith.** 1988. *Grammar and Second Language Teaching: A Book of Readings.* Rowley, Mass.: Newbury House.

Salus, P. (ed.) 1969. *On Language: Plato to von Humboldt.* New York: Holt, Rinehart and Winston.

Samelson, W. 1974. *English as a Second Language, Phase One: Let's Converse.* Englewood Cliffs, NJ: Reston.

Samuels, D.D. and **R.J. Griffore.** 1979. 'The Plattsburgh French language immersion program: its influence on intelligence and self-esteem.' *Language Learning* 29:45–52.

Savignon, S. 1972. *Communicative Competence: An Experiment in Foreign Language Teaching.* Montreal: Marcel Didier.

Scarcella, R. 1983. 'Discourse accent in second language performance' in S. Gass and L. Selinker (eds.): *Language Transfer in Language Learning.* Rowley, Mass.: Newbury House.

Scarcella, R. and **L. Perkins.** 1987. 'Shifting gears: Krashen's input hypothesis.' *Studies in Second Language Acquisition* 9:347–53.

Scarcella, R., E. Andersen, and **S. Krashen,** (eds.) (forthcoming) *Developing Communicative Competence in a Second Language.* Rowley, Mass.: Newbury House.

Schachter, J., A.F. Tyson, and F.J. Diffley. 1976. 'Learner intuitions of grammaticality.' *Language Learning* 26:67–76.

Schank, R. and R. Abelson. 1977. *Scripts, Plans, Goals and Understanding*. Hillsdale, NJ: Lawrence Erlbaum.

Schmidt, M. 1980. 'Coordinate structures and language universals in interlanguage.' *Language Learning* 30:397–416.

Schumann, F. and J. Schumann. 1977. 'Diary of a language learner: an introspective study of second language learning' in H.D. Brown, R.H. Crymes, and C.A. Yorio (eds.): *Teaching and Learning: Trends in Research and Practice*. Washington, DC: TESOL.

Schumann, J. 1978a. 'The pidginization hypothesis' in E. Hatch (ed.): *Second Language Acquisition*. Rowley, Mass.: Newbury House.

Schumann, J. 1978b. *The Pidginization Process: A Model for Second Language Acquisition*. Rowley, Mass.: Newbury House.

Schumann, J. 1983. 'Art and science in second language acquisition research.' *Language Learning* 33:49–76.

Scotton, C. and J. Bernsten. 1988. 'Natural conversations as a model for textbook dialogue.' *Applied Linguistics* 9: 372–84.

Scovel, T. 1978. 'The effect of affect on foreign language learning: a review of the anxiety research.' *Language Learning* 28:129–42.

Seliger, H. and M. Long. (eds.) 1983. *Classroom Oriented Research in Second Language Acquisition*. Rowley, Mass.: Newbury House.

Seliger, H. and E. Shohamy. (in press) *Second Language Research Methods*. Oxford: Oxford University Press.

Selinker, L. 1972. 'Interlanguage.' *IRAL* 10:209–31.

Selinker, L., E.E. Tarone, and V. Hanzeli. (eds.) 1981. *English for Academic and Technical Purposes: Studies in Honor of Louis Trimble*. Rowley, Mass.: Newbury House.

Singh, R., A. d'Anglejean, and J. Carroll. 1982. 'Elicitation of inter-English.' *Language Learning* 32:271–88.

Smith, K. 1986. 'The Distribution of Talk: a Preliminary Needs Assessment of Turn-taking Skills in an ESL College Level Discussion Group.' MA Qualifying Paper, ESL Program, University of Minnesota.

Sorensen, K. 1982. 'Modifying an ESP course syllabus and materials through a teacher-planned needs assessment.' *ESL Working Papers, University of Minnesota* 2 (Summer):1–17.

Spolsky, B. 1978. 'Introduction: linguists and language testers' in B. Spolsky (ed.): *Advances in Language Testing, Series 2: Approaches to Language Testing*. Washington, DC: Center for Applied Linguistics.

Spolsky, B. 1986. 'Formulating a theory of second language learning.' *Studies in Second Language Acquisition* 7:269–88.

Stenson, N. 1974. 'Induced errors' in J.H. Schumann and N. Stenson (eds.): *New Frontiers in Second Language Learning*. Rowley, Mass.: Newbury House.

Stolen, M. 1987. 'The effect of affect on interlanguage phonology' in G. Ioup and S. Weinberger (eds.): *Interlanguage Phonology*. Rowley, Mass.: Newbury House.

Strong, M. 1984. 'Integrative motivation: cause or result of successful second language acquisition?' *Language Learning* 34:1–14.

Swales, J. 1976. 'Verb frequencies in English.' *ESPMENA Bulletin* 4:28–31.

Swales, J. (ed.) 1985. *Episodes in English for Special Purposes*. Oxford: Pergamon Press.

Swan, M. and B. Smith. (eds.) 1987. *Learner English*. Cambridge: Cambridge University Press.

Tarone, E.E. 1979. 'Interlanguage as chameleon.' *Language Learning* 29:181–91.
Tarone, E.E. 1983. 'On the variability of interlanguage systems.' *Applied Linguistics* 4:142–63.
Tarone, E.E. 1984. 'Teaching strategic competence in the foreign language classroom' in S. Savignon and M. Berns (eds.): *Initiatives in Communicative Language Teaching*. Reading, Mass.: Addison-Wesley.
Tarone, E.E. 1985. 'Variability in interlanguage use: a study of style-shifting in morphology and syntax.' *Language Learning* 35:373–404.
Tarone, E.E. 1988. *Variation in Interlanguage*. London: Edward Arnold.
Tarone, E.E., S. Dwyer, S. Gillette, and V. Icke. 1981. 'On the use of the passive in two astrophysics journal papers.' *The ESP Journal* 1:123–40.
Tarone, E.E., U. Frauenfelder, and L. Selinker. 1976. 'Systematicity/variability and stability/instability in interlanguage systems' in H.D. Brown (ed.): *Papers in Second Language Acquisition (Language Learning* Special Issue No. 4:93–134).
Tarone, E.E. and G. Yule. 1987. 'Communication strategies in East–West interactions' in L. Smith (ed.): *Discourse across Cultures*. Oxford: Pergamon Press.

Upshur, J. 1983. 'Measurement of individual differences and explanation in the language sciences.' *Language Learning* 33:99–140.

Vigil, N. and J. Oller. 1976. 'Rule fossilization: a tentative model.' *Language Learning* 26:281–96.

Widdowson, H.G. 1978. *Teaching Language as Communication*. Oxford: Oxford University Press.
Widdowson, H.G. 1979. *Explorations in Applied Linguistics*. Oxford: Oxford University Press.
Widdowson, H.G. 1980. 'Models and fictions.' *Applied Linguistics* 1:165–70.
Widdowson, H.G. 1981. 'English for specific purposes: criteria for course design' in Selinker, Tarone, and Hanzeli (eds.) 1981.
Widdowson, H.G. 1983. *Learning Purpose and Language Use*. Oxford: Oxford University Press.
Williams, M. 1988. 'Language taught for meetings and language used in meetings: is there anything in common?' *Applied Linguistics* 9:145–58.
Wolfson, N. 1981. 'Compliments in cross-cultural perspective.' *TESOL Quarterly* 15:117–24.
Wolfson, N. 1986. 'Research methodology and the question of validity.' *TESOL Quarterly* 20:689–700.
Wolfson, N. and E. Judd. (eds.) 1983. *Sociolinguistics and Language Acquisition*. Rowley, Mass.: Newbury House.
Woods, A., P. Fletcher, and A. Hughes. 1986. *Statistics in Language Studies*. Cambridge: Cambridge University Press.

Yalden, J. 1987. *Principles of Course Design for Language Teaching*. Cambridge: Cambridge University Press.
Yanz, J. 1984. 'The application of the theory of signal detection to the assessment of speech perception.' *Ear and Hearing* 5:64–71.
Yule, G. 1982. 'The objective assessment of aspects of spoken English.' *World Language English* 1:193–9.

Yule, G. 1986. 'Comprehensible notions.' *Applied Linguistics* 7:275–83.

Yule, G., J. Damico, and P. Hoffman. 1987. 'Learners in transition: evidence from the interaction of accuracy and self-monitoring skill in a listening task.' *Language Learning* 37:511–21.

Yule, G. and W. Gregory. 1989. 'Using survey-interviews to foster interactive language learning.' *English Language Teaching Journal* 43.

Yule, G., P. Hoffman, and J. Damico. 1987. 'Paying attention to pronunciation: the role of self-monitoring in perception.' *TESOL Quarterly* 21:765–8.

Yule, G. and E.E. Tarone. (forthcoming) 'Eliciting the performance of strategic competence' in Scarcella, Andersen, and Krashen (eds.).

Yule, G., J. Yanz, and A. Tsuda. 1985. 'Investigating aspects of the language learner's confidence: an application of theory of signal detection.' *Language Learning* 35:473–88.

Zuengler, J. 1989. 'Identity and IL development and use.' *Applied Linguistics* 10:79–95.

Appendices

Appendix 1

Informal needs assessment

Student assignment: assessing your needs for writing in your field (from Hanges 1982)

Assignment

Each of you will do an informal needs assessment of the type of writing you must do in your field of study at the University of Minnesota. Your findings will be presented in the form of a report.

Purpose

In doing this needs assessment, you will find out how much writing is required of you, and you will discover what kind of writing you will have to do. Although it might be impossible to find out about every writing assignment you will have in your graduate program, you should be able to get a general idea of the major types of writing that are required of you.

Procedure

In order to get the most accurate picture of the kinds of writing assignments you will have, it is best that you consult as many sources as possible. It is recommended that you talk not only to professors but also to other students. You may also want to ask the department secretary for additional information on degree requirements. Listed below are some suggested steps:

1. Make sure that you have all of the current information on degree requirements. If you are working toward a master's degree, are you on Plan A or Plan B? If you are a Ph.D. candidate, do you have to submit a proposal for your thesis? Are there courses on writing that your program offers?

2. Make an appointment to see your advisor or another professor. Ask him/her to tell you as much as (s)he can about the writing you will have to do in required courses. Listed below are some of the kinds of writing usually done in academic classes. Ask your advisor which of these you will have to do as a graduate student at this university. Also try to find out which of these you will do more frequently than others.

   summaries and abstracts of books and journal articles
   critical reviews of books and/or journal articles
   research papers that use secondary sources (literature reviews)
   lab/experimental reports

annotated bibliographies
proposals
problem-solving projects or reports
answers to essay questions on tests
MA qualifying papers
Master's thesis
Ph.D. thesis
other types of writing (these are often field specific)

3. Ask the professor if (s)he has examples of the types of writing assignments that you can see.

4. Also ask the professor if there is a recommended style guide that you should use when writing papers. A style guide is a source that explains what form footnotes and bibliography entries should take. Sometimes professors have condensed style guides that they hand out to students; ask the professor if (s)he has one of these that you could have.

5. Find out from your advisor or from someone else if there is a file of old tests that you can look at. If such a file is available, try to get a copy of one or two tests or copy down some representative test questions.

6. Talk to foreign and American students about writing assignments in your program. Students can provide you with information about how difficult assignments are and how long they take to do. They may also have examples of writing assignments that you can see.

The report

All of the information that you collect will be presented in a report. How this report should be written and the form that it should take will be discussed in class at a later date.

Keep in mind that you are collecting this information primarily for your own benefit. However, because your report will be read by other people in this class and by ESL teachers who want to know more about academic writing assignments, it is important that you do a thorough job of collecting data for this report.

Suggested outline for your report

1. Introduction
   (a) Subject
   (b) Purpose
   (c) Brief outline of the rest of the report

2. Body
   (a) Who you interviewed
   (b) What you asked
   (c) What they said
       i Type of writing you will do
       ii Frequency (how often) of each type
   (d) Examples of writing assignments or test questions that you have collected
   (e) How familiar you are with each type of writing

3. Conclusion
   (a) Briefly summarize what you said in (c) and (e) in the body of your report.
   (b) Tell what types of writing you will have to concentrate on most.

Example of a student's report on his own needs for English writing skills (from Hanges 1982)

Civil engineering

The report concerns typical writing that students of civil engineering need to do during their graduate studies. It is believed that this report will make writing of these reports easier because the author will be able to concentrate his attention on the specific kinds of writing that are required in the author's field of study.

The rest of the paper is going to deal with types, frequency, volume, and arrangement of the writing.

The sources of presented information are:

1. Interview with Professor X, author's temporary faculty advisor (types and frequency of writing)
2. Interview with Professor Y (volume and arrangement of writing)
3. General Information Bulletin for Graduate Students, Department of Civil and Mineral Engineering (difference between the thesis of Plan A and B)
4. Orientation lecture for graduate students of civil engineering (difference between the thesis of Plan A and B)

The most frequent types of writing are:

1. Reports on original research
2. Bibliographies
3. Research papers using secondary sources
4. Master's thesis:
   (a) Plan A, or
   (b) Plan B (kind of research report)

Less frequent types of writing are:

1. Summaries of readings
2. Summaries of lectures
3. Book reviews
4. Critiques of journal articles
5. Proposals
6. Preliminary written examination for the Ph.D. degree
7. Ph.D. dissertation

Average volume of some kinds of the writing are shown in the table below:

Kind of writing	Approximate number of pages (without computer data)
Research paper (for 3 credits)	20
Master's thesis: Plan B	50
Plan A	100
Ph.D. dissertation	300

One side of each sheet of the writing is blank. Most of the research papers contain computer printouts.

Typical arrangement of MS thesis or Ph.D. dissertation is as follows:

1. Acknowledgments
2. Contents, list of figures, list of tables
3. Introduction
4. Background (it occupies approximately 25 per cent of the volume)
5. Body of the writing (diagrams are included in the body)
6. Evaluation of applied theories, practical applications, conclusion, suggestions
7. Photographs (if included)
8. Appendixes (if included)
9. References

For further studies the most promising source of information seems to be Professor Y and the rest of the faculty. Fellow students asked about the subject failed to give any information.

Appendix 2

Supermarket story

Exercise 1

Here is a set of four drawings numbered 1 to 4, showing a series of events. Look over the drawings and work out what happened. Then, describe briefly what happened, as if you had been *a witness* to the events and had to provide *an account for someone who had not seen what happened*.

1

2

3

4

Exercise 2

Each student is:
1. provided with the material (picture story and instructions) shown in Exercise 1.
2. sent out, as homework, to find at least one native speaker to be a subject who is then asked, appropriately and persuasively, to follow the instructions and write a short narrative.
3. to read over the elicited narrative and find which expressions the subject used for the different characters and actions.
4. to bring this material to class and add those expressions to a master diagram (on blackboard or overhead transparency) which contains the expressions collected by all students from their subjects.
5. to work out what are the most common expressions used by the subjects, and construct one basic version of the narrative.
6. to discuss any odd expressions they found and any interesting experiences they had when trying to gather their data.

Exercise 3

A week or two after conducting Exercise 2, provide some students with a cassette recorder, a cassette tape, a microphone, and the same picture story used in the first exercise. Send them out to return to the same subjects from whom they elicited written narratives and, this time, to request a spoken version of the same series of events, under the same eye-witness conditions.

The students have to bring their recordings to class and, as a dictation exercise, the whole class has to transcribe the spoken accounts. These transcriptions can then be used as a basis for comparing spoken versus written forms used by the same individual speakers, and for general comparisons between speech and writing (for example, how is speech punctuated?). A discussion of the interesting or frustrating experiences the students had when trying to collect spoken data should also be possible.

Appendix 3

Grammaticality judgment exercise (relative clauses)

Instructions

Some of these sentences are grammatically correct and some of them are incorrect. For each sentence that is correct, circle 'OK'. For each sentence that is incorrect, circle 'NOT OK'. Then, take each sentence that you marked 'NOT OK' and change it to make it correct. You can add words or change the words. For example:

OK/NOT OK   That boy <u>was</u> ill yesterday.

OK/NOT OK   1. The teachers who were coming by bus arrived late.

OK/NOT OK   2. The robber who chased to the parking lot escaped in a blue car.

OK/NOT OK   3. The man was sitting next to me talked a lot about the weather.

OK/NOT OK   4. The driver stopped by the police had to show his license.

OK/NOT OK   5. The passengers who were taken to the airport had to carry their own bags.

OK/NOT OK   6. The doctors working in that hospital didn't have much free time.

OK/NOT OK   7. The woman was surprised by the noise ran out into the street.

OK/NOT OK   8. The student listening to his radio didn't hear the bell.

OK/NOT OK   9. The girl who watching television laughed a lot.

OK/NOT OK 10. The travelers were lost in the forest couldn't find a way out.

OK/NOT OK 11. The professors who teaching those courses gave a lot of assignments.

OK/NOT OK 12. The nurse who was left in charge fell asleep during the night.

OK/NOT OK 13. The men sent to repair the house didn't bring any tools.

OK/NOT OK 14. The people were leaving that night packed their bags early.

OK/NOT OK 15. The children who allowed to leave early got home before the storm.

OK/NOT OK 16. The boy who was waiting outside had a broken arm.

Appendix 4

Tape-recording interaction by learners

Exercise 1

Preparation

Students together choose a topic for the interview and, with the teacher, prepare a series of questions to ask during the interview. One example was: 'What do you (and your family) do on the weekend?'

As a group, the class came up with a number of questions to be used by the interviewer. They also prepared a way of introducing themselves and their purpose. (The students wanted to have their questions on a written survey sheet, for reference.)

Interview sheet

Excuse me. I am doing a project for my English language class. Would you help me by answering a few questions? (*if 'Yes'*) Thank you. (*Switch on cassette recorder.*)

1. Are you married? (*if 'Yes'*) Do you have children? (*if 'Yes'*) How many?
2. Do you work during the weekend? (*if 'Yes'*) What kind of work do you do?
3. Do you go shopping during the weekend?
4. Do you go to church?
5. Do you have any favorite sports? (*if 'Yes'*) What are they?
6. Do you watch TV? (*if 'Yes'*) Which programs do you like?
7. What kind of food do you eat on the weekend?
8. How did you spend last weekend?

Discussion

In class, the students play their recorded interviews and compile, on the blackboard, a general set of the answers to their questions.
Discussion of the data can go in several directions:

1. *On content*: What, if any, is the general pattern of how Americans spend their weekends? How does this differ from the students' weekend activities, both in the US and when they were in their native countries?

2. *On language*: What form do the answers typically take? Are they one word, short phrase, or complete sentences? Were there difficulties understanding some of the answers? What form did the student's questions and responses take?

3. *On the interaction*: What kind of person was interviewed (for example, male/female; younger/older; co-operative or not; impatient or not; accommodating or not, etc.). What kind of misunderstandings arose? What differences were there between this interview and previous interviews (or television interviews, for example)? Which participant was in control (all or part of the time)? Was there a status difference between the participants?

4. *On the interview process*: What problems did the students experience? How would they do things differently next time? What is the next aspect of American life they'd like to find out about?

Warning

For many students, this type of exercise creates substantial communicative stress, especially the first time it is undertaken. That is, although the students are ostensibly in control of the interaction, they are talking to strangers in a role that may be quite novel for them. Consequently, the interview may not always go exactly as planned. We include a transcript of one interview as illustration of the type of data elicited, for teachers who plan to use this type of activity.

Transcript of Korean ESL student (**J**) interviewing an American woman (**A**), in a grocery store near Louisiana State University

J: this interview is a project for my speech class—hi.
A: hello
J: are you single or married?
A: married
J: married
A: uhuh
J: how many children do you have?
A: one child
J: one child—son or—daughter?
A: son
J: son
A: uhuh
J: do you work on Sunday?
A: no—no
J: go to church?—do you go to the church?
A: to church—yes
J: which church?
A: the—em—Episcopal Chapel on campus
J: yeah—eh—I go to the (inaudible)
A: what?
J: Korean Baptist Church
A: Baptist Church?
J: yeah—I went there this morning—
A: uhuh
J: have you favorite sports?
A: my favorite sports?
J: yeah
A: football

J: football
A: yes
J: do you watch football on TV?
A: yes
J: aha—what kind of food you like?
A: what kind of food?
J: yes
A: hamburgers
J: hamburgers?
A: yes
J: and your husband?
A: same
J: same
A: he likes—he likes steak better—steak
J: and your son?
A: he'll eat most anything—he loves—he loves food
J: aha (laughter)—you go shopping—on the weekend?
A: yes
J: where do you go—for shopping?
A: mm—usually K-mart
J: K-mart?
A: yes
J: do you—how do you—em—how do you spend—your weekend?
A: em—with very careful time management—very careful time management—washing clothes—getting all the business taken care of and then if there's time left over watch a good football game
J: em—thank you
A: you're welcome—good luck on your—
J: thank you
A: on your presentation

Exercise 2

Preparation

Students volunteer to try to tape-record a conversation they will have with a native speaker. Planning for this mostly involves discussion of the technical difficulties of getting someone to talk to, especially while being tape-recorded. Informal environments such as the student union coffee shop or around the kitchen table in the house where students are staying with American families have been successful locations. Successful topics which we have found include 'local food', 'the local football/basketball team's performance'· and 'the problems with local weather'.

Discussion

Since this type of data is brought to class by an individual student, that individual is given responsibility for introducing the recording, explaining any background information requested by the group, and clarifying parts of the recording which may be unclear or (with the teacher's help) unfamiliar vocabulary or expressions. The focus, in this case, is on making sense of what was said, where misunderstandings seem to occur (and why), and how the participants were accommodating to each other. The best initial activity is to treat the recording as the basis of an informal dictation exercise, with students allowed to ask for repetition, clarification, spelling of unusual names, etc..

Warning

For teachers planning to use an exercise of this type, we should point out that the data is inevitably highly localized, both in terms of content and language. In the following fragment, the native speaker (F) has a strong southern Louisiana accent and uses a lot of local terms for food.

Partial transcript of a Japanese ESL student (M) talking to an American woman (F) in her Baton Rouge home about local food

M: What kind of food do you like?
F: I like the Cajun food the best
M: mm—aha—now—what is the Cajun food?
F: it's—em—food that—is made by the French-speaking people in Louisiana—and—it's usually—seafood
M: aha
F: and it's highly seasoned and usually served with rice or em—some of the dishes are
M: ah—now—what typical Cajun—what is a typical Cajun food is?
F: oh like eh one of my favorite ones is gumbo—and that's em made with any kind of seafood you can put lots of different kind of seafood in it
M: ah
F: crawfish and shrimp and crab—but you can also make it with turkey and chicken—sausage—and usually em you serve it in a big bowl with rice
M: I see—and do you eat—any other Cajun food?
F: yes em crawfish étouffé—and that's made with crawfish tails—
M: aha
F: and you cook that down with—eh—onions and bell pepper and celery and you serve that on top of rice also
M: aha—I already ate—the other one—I ate the eh—Jambalaya
F: Jambalaya that's good too
M: eh spicy food is ah—very typical one
F: yes very typical of Cajun food—in fact my husband is from Ohio— and when we married I said to him—I'd like to learn how to cook some of the things that your mother had always cooked for you all of your life—
M: aha
F: and he says no please learn to cook like your mother cause she cooks Cajun food (laughter)—so that's what I cook a lot of ...

Appendix 5

Description tasks

Procedure

The speaker sees only one object (on video or in a photograph) and is instructed to describe that object so that the listener can identify the object from a set of similar objects.

The listener has a set of three photographs, labeled A, B, and C, and, following the speaker's description, has to choose which one of the photographed objects is being described.

For teachers interested in creating simple tasks of this type, we illustrate some of our prompts in the following four exercises. In each case, the speaker saw only one (photographed) object from each of these sets seen by the listener. Of course, the speaker could not see the listener's photographs.

Exercise 1

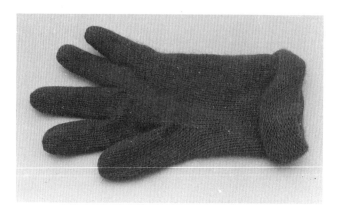

A

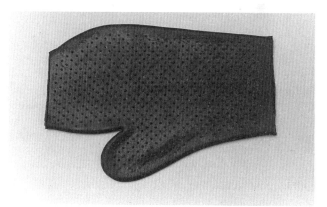

B

C

Exercise 2

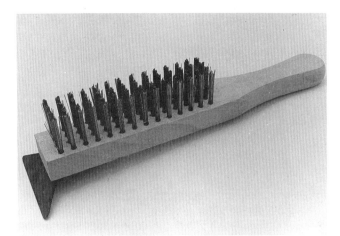

A

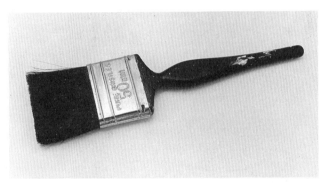

B

C

Exercise 3

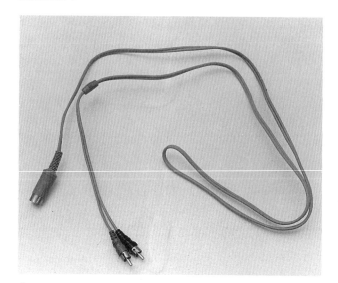

A

B

C

Exercise 4

A

B

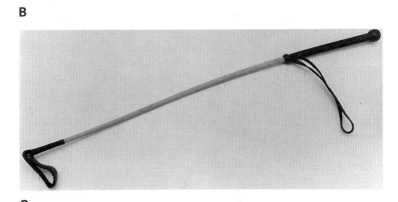

C

Appendix 6

Assembly tasks

Procedure

The speaker watches, on video, a piece of equipment being assembled or some procedure being carried out and then has to provide an account of the process for the listener.

The listener is provided with a set of six photographs related to the process which is seen on video by the speaker. Some of the photographs depict steps in the process, others do not. The listener, following the speaker's account, has to choose only those photographs which depict steps in the process described by the speaker.

For teachers interested in creating comparable tasks, the following two sets of listeners' photographs, and accompanying transcripts of speakers' accounts, will provide illustrations.

The Christmas tree stand

Speaker's account

Since we cannot illustrate the videotape seen by the speaker, we have provided a transcript of a native Hebrew speaker describing the assembly of the Christmas tree stand. The reader may use this as a basis for carrying out the accompanying listener's task.

at first there was eh—some kind of eh—eh round metal—I'm not sure that it's metal I think so eh it is—three holes but three of them were—em more important—eh—in one in one of the three holes—the man eh put—some kind of metal em—a metal piece which was long and thin—and after putting the three eh pieces of metal he connected them—by another eh metal piece which made from—from some kind of metal also and he connected them in a way that all all of the three—all the three edges of these pieces three pieces were—were covered—by this eh—round metal and after doing it he—tried to he put some eh—some nails in all of this these eh metal pieces—just in order to—to strengthen

Listener's task

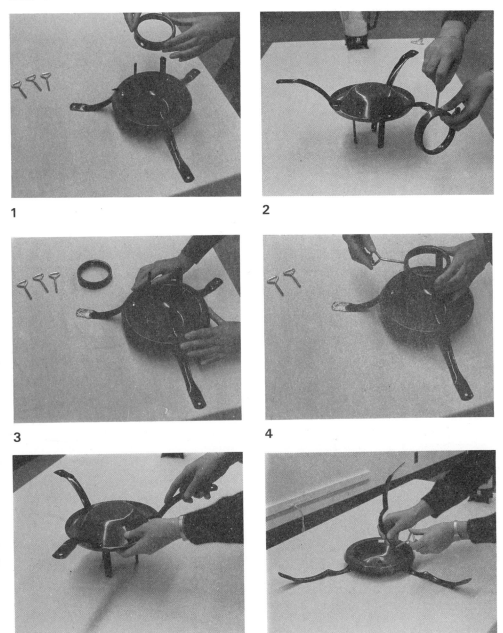

Making coffee

Speaker's account

The following is a transcript of a native Chinese speaker describing one method of making coffee. As with the Christmas tree stand transcript above, the reader may use this as a basis for carrying out the accompanying listener's task.

I guess this is—the—uh—make coffee—on the coffee pot (laugh) I call coffee pot—first put one cup of coffee in—from the grass—glass—to the coffee pot—then nn—pour—uh—pour—of the water in the —nn—pot—and uh—then put on the—uh—then—use something—uh—scrub—something—stir—stir—then nn—put the—cover—nn—the cover is a special kind of cover—and—uh—then push the —uh—cover—nn—push the cover—uh—abou—above of the cover—other part sinks—push—then coffee—you can drink—this coffee

Listener's task

1

2

3

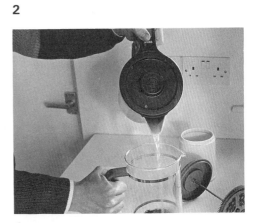

4

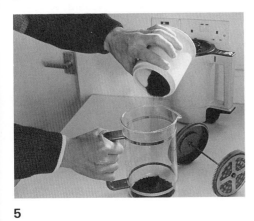

5

6

Appendix 7
Narrative tasks

Procedure

The speaker watches, on video, a brief series of events and then has to tell the listener what happened.

The listener is provided with a set of six photographs related to the events which are seen on video by the speaker. Some of the photographs show scenes from the story, others do not. The listener, following the speaker's narrative, has to choose only those photographs which depict scenes in the story narrated by the speaker.

For teachers interested in creating comparable tasks, the following two sets of listeners' photographs, and accompanying transcripts of speakers' accounts, will provide illustrations.

The magazine story

Speaker's account

Since we cannot illustrate the videotape seen by the speaker, we have provided a transcript of a native Korean speaker's version of the magazine story. The reader may use this as a basis for carrying out the accompanying listener's task.

this situation was happened in classroom—some womans—woman teachers came into the classroom—but there is nobody yet—so he got uh many materials for lecture—including a magazine—and he put—he put—uh desk—and she wroit—wrote down something—wrote in in—board—she wrote something—and then—uh one woman student came in the classroom and uh take a seat—front of that—uh like uh lecterums—lecturums—and—she look—look at the uh magazine—of the teacher's magazine—and he look at—and uh he put uh the magazine on his chair his desk on her desk—uh under the—uh her purshu—purshe—purshu?—purshu?—and put the magazine on the—her purshu and go out the—classroom—and then the other—the other woman student came in the classroom—and sit next—next to a woman's the woman's—chair—chairs—and she looked uh to woman's uh magazine—maybe she she confused—misunderstand—this magazine is uh—the woman student's—not teacher's—so she put into the—her purshet—not on the purshet—put into the her purshet—so—and at that time again she came back—so there are two woman students in classroom—and then—maybe the lecture is beginning—and the lecturer needed the magazine—but—when he look—find—search for the magazine he can't find—so he he's continue—look uh—search for the magazine—and surround the desk—under the floors—uh—it's the situation

Listener's task

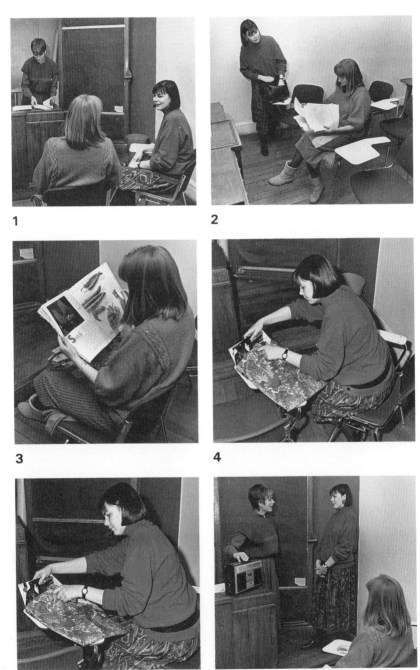

1

2

3

4

5

6

The drawing on the blackboard

Speaker's account

The following is a transcript of a native Spanish speaker's version of the blackboard drawing story.

the teacher—was writing—and drawing three—geometric figures—the the circle circle triangle and—es—esquare when they—had just—had just finished —the triangle remembered something important and said to a student wait a moment—I need to go out and when they go out of the classroom—one student stand up and write in the circle a funny face—after the another student say I can draw—something fun too—and standing up and draw with the triangle arms and legs and—put hair an ugly face to the circle—when they the—another student stand up—in this moment the teacher—coming into the classroom and—say what happened—what happened with my explication and my drawing and blame to the student for this—this wrong way and another student say I didn't—and blame to another student

Listener's task

1

2

3

4

5

6

Appendix 8

Communication strategy classwork (from Nelson 1989)

Exercise 1. Communication strategies: Introduction

A *strategy* is a method or technique for doing something. *Communication strategies* are techniques for communicating, especially when communication is difficult, as it is in a foreign language.

Consider these examples of communication strategies at work. In each of them **A** is an American and **B** is a person who is learning English as a second language.

Example 1

(In **B**'s pronunciation, *sell* and *sail* sound the same. We will represent both as s---l.)

B: My uncle is going to s---l his boat this weekend.
A: Oh, has he a sailboat?
B: Yes.
A: Are you going with him this weekend?
B: Uh—no, he's going to s---l the boat.
A: Yeah, I understand. Are you going sailing with him?
B: No, I'm sorry. S---l, not s---l. Someone is going to buy his boat.
A: Oh, he's *selling* the boat! I got it!

Example 2

(In **B**'s speech *slept* and *slipped* sound the same. We will represent both as sl----.)

B: I sl---- on the floor last night.
A: Oh, did you hurt yourself?
B: Well, uh ... not really. It wasn't very comfortable, I guess.
A: Why was the floor slippery?
B: Oh, no ... I don't think you understand. I sl---- on the floor!
A: You fell, right?
B: No, I sl---- on the floor. I don't have any furniture yet, no bed or anything.
A: Oh! You *slept* on the floor! I understand now!

Example 3

(**B** doesn't know the word *frisbee.*)

A: Do you have frisbees in your country?

B: Fris...? I don't think I know the word.

A: Frisbee. You throw it, it's like a plate, made of plastic. People play catch with it on the beach sometimes.

B: Oh, yes, we have them! What's the word again?

A: Frisbee.

B: Frisbee. Yes, we have frisbees.

Example 4

(B doesn't remember the word *pet*.)

A: There aren't many kids in my neighborhood, so my daughter doesn't have anyone to play with.

B: Maybe she needs a, a, a ...

A: A pen pal?

B: No, a, a, a dog or a cat to play with, some kind of animal?

A: Yeah, well, that's a good idea, but our apartment building doesn't allow pets.

Example 5

(B cannot recall the past tense of *take*.)

A: Where did you park your car?

B: No, I didn't drive. I don't have a car ...

A: You walked?

B: No, I, I, I ... bus.

A: Oh, yeah. I took the bus too.

Exercise 2. Communication strategies: Giving more information

Follow the example.

A: What's your favorite *color*?

B: (pretending not to understand the part in italics) I'm sorry. I don't quite understand. My favorite what?

A: What's your favorite color—blue? Red? Green? (A uses the strategy of giving more information—here, in the form of examples of colors, or possible answers to the question.)

1. What *sport* do you like best?
2. Do you have a *pet*?
3. Do you have any *hobbies*?
4. What's your favorite *time of year*?
5. How's *the weather* in Washington at this time of year?
6. What *subject* did you like best when you were in high school?
7. Have you ever been to any *cities in the eastern US*?
8. What *kind of transportation* do you use to go to school?
9. What is your favorite *month*?
10. Have you visited any *European countries*?
11. Do you play any *musical instruments*?
12. Where can I buy *jewelry*?
13. Do you want your son to go to *college*?
14. What *time of day* do you like best for working?

15. What do you think is the safest *way to travel*?
16. Where can I buy *dishes*?
17. Is the governor of your state very *ambitious*?
18. Have you ever seen a *swan*?
19. Do you have a *coin* in your pocket?
20. Do you have *anything to read*?
21. What *other states* have you visited?
22. Do you eat *meat*?
23. What *kind of movies* do you like?
24. Where can I buy *sports equipment*?
25. Do you like *fruit*?
26. Have you ever worked for *a big company*?
27. Who is your favorite *singer*?
28. Which *region of the US* is the best place for raising a family?
29. Do your students know any *irregular verbs*?
30. Have you ever read a book about *American presidents*?
31. What *textbook* do you use for your classes in Japan?
32. Who is your favorite *actress*?

Appendix 9

Exercises used for self-monitoring study

Classroom exercise (Yule, Yanz, and Tsuda 1985)

Transcript of tape

Part 1

1. When did they fire him?
2. He is always late for class.
3. It was a big lock.
4. He was banished from Russia.
5. Every cloud has a silver lining.
6. That man is very sick.
7. What did you fear?
8. Can the Soviets play the game by their own rules?
9. He used to be a pirate.
10. I found the story wordy.
11. I met Joan yesterday.
12. I ate a hot dog with mustard.
13. Don't lean on a reed.
14. He picked up a pin.
15. It couldn't be in sight because of the confusion.
16. Give me a seat.
17. She went to the palace.
18. She tampered with the jury.
19. He was detained by business.
20. It was a nice hut.
21. The Japanese eat bean curd.
22. The doctor gave me the bill.
23. There was a red pen on the kitchen table.
24. Tanaka is out on bail.
25. The bird picked insects out of the tree bark.

Part 2

26. **A:** Hey, John, did you pass the test?
    B: You must be joking.
27. **A:** Hey, Bill, it's snowing outside!
    B: So, what else is new?

28. **A:** Hello Karen.
    B: Hi, do you have a minute?
29. **A:** Didn't you go to the concert last night, Ann?
    B: Uh-huh.
30. **A:** When can I come to your office?
    B: How about eleven o'clock, Mary?
    A: Couldn't be better.

Student answer sheet

Part 1

	Completely sure			Not sure at all	
1. *fire/hire*	5	4	3	2	1
2. *rate/late*	5	4	3	2	1
3. *lock/rock*	5	4	3	2	1
4. *banished/vanished*	5	4	3	2	1
5. *crowd/cloud*	5	4	3	2	1
6. *sick/thick*	5	4	3	2	1
7. *fear/hear*	5	4	3	2	1
8. *play/pray*	5	4	3	2	1
9. *pilot/pirate*	5	4	3	2	1
10. *worthy/wordy*	5	4	3	2	1
11. *John/Joan*	5	4	3	2	1
12. *mustard/master*	5	4	3	2	1
13. *reed/lead*	5	4	3	2	1
14. *pin/bin*	5	4	3	2	1
15. *insight/in sight*	5	4	3	2	1
16. *seat/sheet*	5	4	3	2	1
17. *Paris/palace*	5	4	3	2	1
18. *tempered/tampered*	5	4	3	2	1
19. *detained/retained*	5	4	3	2	1
20. *hut/hat*	5	4	3	2	1
21. *card/curd*	5	4	3	2	1
22. *pill/bill*	5	4	3	2	1
23. *pen/pan*	5	4	3	2	1
24. *bail/veil*	5	4	3	2	1
25. *picked/pecked*	5	4	3	2	1

Part 2

	Completely sure			Not sure at all	

26. (a) John is sure he passed.
    (b) John is not sure if he passed or not.   5 4 3 2 1
    (c) John is sure he did not pass.

27. (a) Bill is interested in what he hears.
    (b) Bill is not interested in what he hears.   5 4 3 2 1
    (c) Bill wants to hear more about this.

28. (a) Karen wants to discuss something.
    (b) Karen is asking what time it is.   5 4 3 2 1
    (c) Karen is too busy to talk.

29. (a) Ann went to the concert.
    (b) Ann didn't go to the concert.   5 4 3 2 1
    (c) Ann doesn't want to answer the question.

30. (a) Mary thinks eleven o'clock is the worst time.
    (b) Mary thinks eleven o'clock is the best time.   5 4 3 2 1
    (c) Mary is afraid she won't be able to come at
        eleven o'clock.

Part 3   **Completely**   **Not sure**
                                           sure   **at all**

31. She gave me ____ good   *a*
    advice.   *some*   5 4 3 2 1
                               a few

32. I have three books.   *other*
    One is mine and ____   *the others*   5 4 3 2 1
    are yours.   *the other*

33. She has lived there ____   *for*
    1980.   *since*   5 4 3 2 1
                               by

34. I looked forward to   *hear*
    ____ you.   *heard*   5 4 3 2 1
                               hearing

35. The building ____ he   *which*
    lives is very old.   *that*   5 4 3 2 1
                               where

36. If I ____ enough time   *have*
    now, I would write to   *had*   5 4 3 2 1
    my parents.   *would have*

37. I don't know where   *he lives*
    ____.   *does he live*   5 4 3 2 1
                               lives he

38. The news in that   *is*
    magazine ____ two   *are*   5 4 3 2 1
    weeks old.   *were*

39. She ran, otherwise she   *would miss*
    ____ her bus.   *missed*   5 4 3 2 1
                               would have missed

40. This one is more ____   *better*
    than that one.   *old*   5 4 3 2 1
                               important

Part 4

		Completely sure				Not sure at all
41. The doctor ____ me to get plenty of rest.	*said* *told* *spoke*	5	4	3	2	1
42. Mary is ____ her brother.	*alike* *like* *look like*	5	4	3	2	1
43. It was an ____ movie.	*exciting* *excited* *excites*	5	4	3	2	1
44. I ____this radio from my country.	*brought* *took* *gave*	5	4	3	2	1
45. I have ____ the piano for one year.	*exercised* *trained* *practiced*	5	4	3	2	1
46. This is the picture she ____.	*wrote* *typed* *drew*	5	4	3	2	1
47. She ____ me an umbrella.	*borrowed* *took* *lent*	5	4	3	2	1
48. She will ____ him a good wife.	*turn* *make* *become*	5	4	3	2	1
49. He is very ____.	*considerate* *considering* *consider*	5	4	3	2	1
50. He is ____ a mustache.	*taking* *raising* *growing*	5	4	3	2	1

Listening exercise

Transcript of tape

Practice examples:
a: What did you see?
b: I wanted a new cap.
c: He told us about the bang.

Now begin.

1. It was a really small hut.
2. There was a ship in the picture.
3. You need to get a good lather.
4. Don't worry about the ban.
5. They said the launch would be later.
6. The sherry was delicious.
7. There was only one small rib.
8. It was a very big lock.
9. I met Joan yesterday.
10. When did he leave there?
11. They said the boss was late.
12. It was an oddly-shaped nut.
13. We saw a very big cloud.
14. We found a narrow pass.
15. Can you feel it?
16. He loathes all those boxes.
17. Can you believe it's a frog?
18. She wanted to sell her boat.
19. We knew he wouldn't suit her.
20. They always ate a large breakfast.
21. We'll soon get a saw.
22. The boy's nickname was Tad.
23. Do something before the man's deaf.
24. Everyone was pleasant.
25. He didn't want to hit the water.
26. Please don't turn over your cuffs.
27. There's no problem with their breeding.
28. Just put that stuff in the back.
29. She wouldn't talk about his rages.
30. Someone stole the coat.
31. He's going to buy a wrench.
32. The prize was really good.
33. He believed in his fate.
34. The man arrived on time.
35. Which plays did you see?
36. I thought he was choking.
37. I told him it wasn't wine.
38. He was looking for a cap.
39. Look at those pretty baubles.
40. Please sand it carefully.

Student answer sheet

You will hear forty sentences on the tape. In each sentence, you have to identify one of the words spoken and put a circle round the word you hear. Then, choose one number on the scale to indicate how sure you are that your answer is correct. Here are some practice examples.

		Very sure		Not sure at all
(a) What did you ____?	*say/see*	3	2	1
(b) I wanted a new ____.	*car/cap*	3	2	1
(c) He told us about the ____.	*bang/bank*	3	2	1

		Very sure		Not sure at all
1.	*hut/hat*	3	2	1
2.	*sheep/ship*	3	2	1
3.	*lather/ladder*	3	2	1
4.	*van/ban*	3	2	1
5.	*launch/lunch*	3	2	1
6.	*sherry/cherry*	3	2	1
7.	*rip/rib*	3	2	1
8.	*rock/lock*	3	2	1
9.	*Joan/John*	3	2	1
10.	*leave/live*	3	2	1
11.	*boss/bus*	3	2	1
12.	*net/nut*	3	2	1
13.	*cloud/crowd*	3	2	1
14.	*path/pass*	3	2	1
15.	*fill/feel*	3	2	1
16.	*loads/loathes*	3	2	1
17.	*frog/frock*	3	2	1
18.	*sail/sell*	3	2	1
19.	*suit/shoot*	3	2	1
20.	*ate/eat*	3	2	1
21.	*thaw/saw*	3	2	1
22.	*Tad/Ted*	3	2	1
23.	*deaf/death*	3	2	1
24.	*pleasant/present*	3	2	1
25.	*hit/heat*	3	2	1
26.	*cups/cuffs*	3	2	1
27.	*breeding/breathing*	3	2	1
28.	*bag/back*	3	2	1
29.	*wages/rages*	3	2	1
30.	*coat/code*	3	2	1
31.	*wrench/ranch*	3	2	1
32.	*prize/price*	3	2	1
33.	*faith/fate*	3	2	1
34.	*men/man*	3	2	1
35.	*plays/place*	3	2	1
36.	*choking/joking*	3	2	1
37.	*wine/mine*	3	2	1
38.	*cap/cab*	3	2	1
39.	*bubbles/baubles*	3	2	1
40.	*sand/send*	3	2	1

Index